PASSION!
RECLAIMING THE FIRE IN YOUR HEART

Roz Van Meter
and
Pat Pearson

Hollingsworth Press

The lines from "i carry your heart with me (i carry it in my heart)" are reprinted from COMPLETE POEMS, 1904-1962, by e.e. cummings, edited by George J. Firmage, by permission of Liveright Publishing Corporation. Copyright © 1952, 1980, 1991 by the Trustees for the e. e. cummings Trust.

Copyright © 1994 by Roz Van Meter and Pat Pearson

All rights reserved
including the right of reproduction
in whole or in part in any form
except by written permission of the copyright holders.
Brief quotations may be used in reviews.
Please send tear sheets of reviews, or direct any inquiries, to

Hollingsworth Press

10914 Listi Drive
Dallas, TX 75238

ISBN: 0-944486-01-0
Library of Congress Catalog Card Number: 94-75608
Includes Index

Cover design by Ginnie Siena Bivona
Photography by Robert Goodman and Don Goldston
Image Enhancement by Donald Wristen
Printed in the United States of America

PASSION!

TABLE OF CONTENTS

INVITATION TO THE PASSION SALON		5
CHAPTER 1:	The Power of Passion	13
CHAPTER 2:	What Is Passion?	19
CHAPTER 3:	Where Does It Come From?	25
CHAPTER 4:	How Do We Lose It?	35
CHAPTER 5:	Focused Passion — "TO DO"	47
CHAPTER 6:	Passion for Life — "TO BE"	63
CHAPTER 7:	The Seven Paths to Passion	71
Path #1:	Honoring Yourself	75
Path #2:	Claiming Your Authentic Power	85
Path #3:	Expanding Your Comfort Zone	99
Path #4:	Following Your Bliss	113
Path #5:	Affirming the YES! to Life	123
Path #6:	Trusting the Inner Click	133
Path #7:	Uniting Your Head and Heart	143
CHAPTER 8:	Passionate Love	151
CHAPTER 9:	The Mind-Body Connection	165
CHAPTER 10:	Coming Alive!	177
EXERCISES		183
READING LIST		

DEDICATIONS

From Roz

To Carl Whitaker, who reveres "personhood."
If personhood is complete and courageous
authenticity, he embodies it for us all.

To Kathryn Van Cooper, whose passion for life
has just begun. May you always live
with open arms and an open heart.

And with wholehearted passionate love
to Robert Goodman.

From Pat

To Steve Frohling.
You reawakened the fire in my heart
and taught me that love does triumph.

INVITATION TO

THE PASSION SALON

You are hereby invited to our
PASSION SALON,
*a lively evening of
conversation and exploration.*

Dear Friends, (the letter said),
We want to tell you about a book we are writing about PASSION and invite you to contribute ideas to it. By PASSION we mean the

ARDOR
    ZEAL
        FERVOR
            EXCITEMENT
                WHOLE-HEARTEDNESS

that accompany a powerful emotional investment in an idea, social cause, creative expression, or relationship—or zest for life.

We want this book to be a collaborative effort by many people. We know your life is very full, but would you be willing to share your thoughts, memories of a passionate experience, favorite books or stories about passionate people? Enclosed is our working outline, to give you some thought-starters. We will deeply appreciate all contributions and will acknowledge you in the book.

THE PASSION PROJECT

From the first exuberant response to the Salons, the Passion Project took on a life of its own. At formal and informal Salons, friends and strangers alike reacted with some version of "What a great idea!" They loved sharing stories of passions loved and lost—not necessarily about love affairs, but rather of times when they burned with life and excitement and hope and—well, with passion.

Each Salon had intense energy, serious thought, and high feelings. The very act of talking about *Passion!* created its own shared passion within each group. Conversation, which seems to have become an endangered species, is alive and well in the Passion Project.

Inquiring minds, we found, want to think—and talk and argue and laugh and remember.

Invitation to the Passion Salon

And now we invite you, too, to take part in the Passion Project. As you read this book,

> **OPEN YOUR HEART**
>
> **AND SAY A-H-H-H.**

Create a Passion Salon of your own with friends, a study group, or just with yourself. Make up your own thought-starting questions or use the ones in this book. You may enjoy one of the most stimulating evenings you've spent in a long time.

If you don't believe it, here are some responses to the question, *"What is passion for you?"* (As is true throughout the book, names have been changed in some instances, but the sentiments are uncensored.)

SARAH: It is a type of energy that doesn't have to be manic. I am a reserved person. People think I am not passionate, but I am. *I think passion is as much feeling for the tap root as reaching for the sky.*

MARY SUE: I have a friend who, when she sees I'm getting burned out or depressed, asks me: *What is important to you, and are you including it in your life?* When I start doing that, I get my passion back. When I don't do it, my energy and motivation and fire diminish until they're almost out.

I enroll people in my passions. I'm very good at that, and I do it the way I am now, with unedited talking. I'm different from Mark that way. He can edit and cut his persuasiveness [as a documentary film producer] and mine is extemporaneous. *I am a work always in progress.*

GERTRUDE: In my opinion, anyone who is absorbed in a passion can get burned out, because you are so intense, so deeply enthralled in whatever you're doing.

I used to be a competent musician. I remember once sitting at the piano and playing, and when I finished, I knew to the depths of my soul that this was perfect. The sound stayed in the room as though it were reluctant to leave. I still get goosebumps thinking of it. That is the kind of *ecstasy* that happens very rarely, and when it does occur, you spend the rest of your life trying to attain it again.

ROBERT: I was born in a small town and raised by wonderful people who were very shy and modest and not really passionate. The family watchword was, "Don't attract attention to yourself. Be a good, steady, solid, honest kind of person."

Maybe that's why I was attracted to a woman with a lot of joy and passion for life.

When the idea of Passion was first brought up, the thing that first came up for me was romantic passion, because that certainly revolutionized my young life when I discovered romance and sex and passion. Then in college I really discovered music in a powerful way, and listening to music like Carmina Burana absolutely transported me to someplace else.

VANESSA: I went off to college when I was barely seventeen, much too immature socially and emotionally. I became very withdrawn and quite depressed, and would not leave my room. An older girl, my "Big Sister," visited me just before Easter and brought me a big bunny that played <u>In Your Easter Bonnet</u>. I liked it but I still didn't want to leave my room.

She put my coat on me and half pushed me down the big ravine and up the other side, into the woods where the snow had not yet melted. There, under a tree, she showed me where the violets were pushing up through the snow.

After forty years, I still weep to think how nearly I came to giving up on life.

For me Passion is the life force, the violets pushing up through the snow.

HOPE: I heard a poem as a small child, and I've never been able to locate it again. It goes,

> **The antiseptic baby and the prophylactic pup**
> **Were playing in the garden when the bunny ambled up.**
> **They looked upon the creature with loathing undisguised:**
> *He wasn't disinfected and he wasn't sterilized.*

I think my family was like that. My brother and I got moulded by guilt, and that has inhibited my passion.

I always loved horses. There's a picture of me at age two, wearing my Davy Crockett hat and riding a stick horse. I remember coming home after thirty-six hours at a horse show, after winning my first trophy, and my mother said, "Yeah, but you missed church."

BARBARA: I feel so totally passionate at all levels, and I think I have since I was a child.

My passion has a solitary piece that has to do with growing up in a large family of very passionate, strong-willed people, most of it negatively expressed. There is a lot of freedom in solitude—I am free to create because it matters to no one. I'm passionate about my tomatoes and my dogs, about my birds, about the book I'm reading.

To me Passion is about process, unattached to outcome. I absolutely believe that there is no security anywhere in the world and I assume that there is no tomorrow. I think I am free to be passionate because every day is sufficient in itself.

ELIZABETH: When the topic of passion came up, it reminded me of a book I picked up with a test about whether you ought to be self-employed. One question was, "Are you passionate?" I never answered the question, but it's stuck with me every since.

When I reflect on what I've done to date, I think that although I may have strong opinions about something, I don't feel strongly enough to get out of my chair and go do something about it.

I came here tonight feeling like I'm lacking passion, but I do have a love for life. I do have passion for experience.

ROZ: That's all we're after, to have people think about passion and define it for themselves, whatever that may be.

It's about waking up and using all your senses, being more alive right now. I just like to see people be at choice in their lives, and it's hard for me to believe that people would deliberately live without passion if they knew they could choose to have it!

❖   ❖   ❖   ❖   ❖

We want to acknowledge the following contributors, as well as those we may have overlooked and the people we never really met, just encountered in passing.

Thank you for your adding your passion to ours.

Jess Alford
Nelda Bayer
Marianne Beckham
Jim Bennight
Barbara Berendzen
Mark Birnbaum
Ginnie Bivona
Carol Bowman
Norm Bowman
Mina Brown
Pete Caudle
Mickey Chandler
L'isle Cooper
Gertrude Croy
Mary Jo Cuny
Phil Cuny
Bill Drake
Susan Ellis
Gladney Flatt
Ed Fordyce
Mary Sue Foster
Judy Freeman
Lynne Godsey
Norm Goldsmith
Carolyn Goldston
Don Goldston
Robert Goodman
Ellen Greenberg
Marty Greenberg

Ray Hetzel
Ernie Hill
Tom Iverson
Jean Johnson
Doug Knabe
Lynn Leight
Dan Loveland
Peg Loveland
Glenn Maddox
John Mitchell
Leslie Murphy
Sarah Norton
Marci Novak
Roberta Nutt
Kathy O'Halloran
Pete Caudle
Maureen Peters
Joyce Reynolds
Alberto Rubio
Carolyn Sedalnick
T. D. Doherty
Calie Travis
Jim Travis
Carol Vesey
John Vesey
Nora Weaver
Carl Whitaker
Reed Whittle
Randall Winter

CHAPTER 1

THE POWER OF PASSION

*Your reward for passion
is the wonderful way it feels to be passionate,
and the incredible things that pour into your life
when you are.*
— **Marianne Williamson**

Passion! It's the fire in the heart, the fire in the belly, the *engagement* with something or someone or life itself.

It's also risky, because it means being ignited in an era when it is not in vogue. We are a society that definitely tends to trends, and today's trend is toward passivity. Sit and watch sitcoms. Watch sports instead of playing. Watch what passes for conversations on talk shows, instead of conversing.

Even when we're in active mode, it's often for the satisfaction of the outcome, not pleasure in the process.

Passion, on the other hand, absolutely <u>loves the process!</u> It isn't just the finished picture that pulls the artist, it's the <u>act of painting</u>.

Above all, passion is about being free. Contrary to myth, passions don't enslave us, they are the fuel that fires our rockets of individuality. We are most alive when we acknowledge, embrace, and enjoy the things or people or openheartedness we love, whether our passions burn fiercely or glow gently.

Everyone has known passion. People who think they haven't simply can't remember that far back, but somewhere, some time in the past, they burned with delight or excitement about something. A rage at a teacher or a sibling, an ardent tenderness for a pet, an indignation at wrongdoings. The two-year-old's rapt absorption in the goings-on of a ladybug.

We need to take a look at how individual people learn to send their passion underground. Perhaps that's how the whole society does it, one person at a time getting overwhelmed by problems or the speed of change or the magnitude of challenges. Ironically, that's just when a person most needs personal passion. It can cut the world down to size. The philatelist marvels at the intricacies of a strange foreign stamp, the choreographer works for ten hours on a three-minute dance routine. They bring shape and meaning and their own brand of exultation to a world they can personally shape.

The authors, Roz and Pat, met sixteen years ago and immediately discovered some things we had in common. We were both therapists with brand-new practices and a shaky hold on the future, but blessed with the ability to enjoy small pleasures.

We also had a similar ironic sense of humor which led us to see the funny or touching or challenging aspect of the predicaments we got ourselves into.

Most of all, both of us (usually) got an enormous kick out of life.

For the past several years, however, we have felt distinctly in the minority. In our offices, at our seminars, even in letters to the editor, we keep hearing and seeing the same theme: disengagement, disillusionment, ennui.

Instead of grabbing life with their bare hands and relishing it, people seem to be handling it with tongs.

We believe that America's lost (or misplaced) passion is a great tragedy, almost of the magnitude of the Great Depression. It reflects a nationwide Hidden Depression that cannot wholly be accounted for by an economic recession or unresponsive government. The sheer vitality, the quality of aliveness that used to set this society apart from the rest of the weary world, appears to be seeping away.

How can our society have strayed so far from passion? Heaven knows our founding fathers had it. How and when did it become fashionable to be cool, to not get involved? To write a check to the Salvation Army kettle instead of adopting a family for Christmas and shopping for them and delivering the gifts ourselves?

Which came first, the apathetic chicken or the dispirited egg? Either way, the whole country seems to be in a malaise of spirit.

The only passion we are regularly made aware of is inflamed madness—horrifically violent movies, a myriad of books about demon possession, real-life murders—in part, we believe, because passion repressed can become passion that ultimately explodes.

> *We advocate a return to*
> *real-life, healthy passion :*
> *selectively chosen, lovingly cultivated,*
> *and fiercely protected.*

Can you remember a time you were passionate about something or someone, or just about being alive? If you have lost your ability to feel passion, do you think it can be relearned?

Were you taught that passion was unseemly, not manly or ladylike or professional or mature? Did you secretly envy or admire a maverick family member, an eccentric great-aunt or legendary great-grandpa who scandalized the clan by following her or his own drummer?

Join us in our inquiry into the nature of passion, its advantages and liabilities. As a force of nature, it usually declines the linear path, so our tracking will probably take us down some curves and switchbacks, but at least it will get us to thinking and perhaps even recapturing ... something ... precious.

Passion rushes forward like fire on a track,
racing wild from someone's heart
as it zigzags into someone or something.
There goes God, fingerpainting again.

— Marianne Williamson

CHAPTER 2

WHAT IS PASSION?

That face on the TV screen glows like a klieg light with passionate joy and the boy's whole body does a puppyish wriggle-dance. The Special Olympics kid has crossed the finish line! He didn't come in first, but to him just finishing the race brings a triumph close to ecstasy.

We sit in the darkened theatre with the big screen and state-of-the-art sound, to see MGM's newly-restored print of <u>Singin' in the Rain.</u> We watch Gene Kelly throw his head back and holler,

GOTTA DANCE !

declaring the passion of all the dancers before and after him who tortured their bodies for years because dancing wasn't just something they wanted to do, it was what they had to do.

Here is that delightful old life-lover, Zorba the Greek, from Nikos Kazantzakis's splendid novel and the subsequent movie:

"What is that mystery?" he asks. "What is a woman, and why does she turn our heads? Just tell me, I ask you, what's the meaning of that?" He interrogates himself with the same amazement when he sees a man, a tree in blossom, a glass of cold water. Zorba sees everything every day as if for the first time.

When his boss refuses to take a risk because he doesn't want any trouble:

"You don't want any trouble!" Zorba exclaimed in stupefaction. "Life IS trouble! Death, no. But to LIVE— do you know what that means?
... "Don't calculate, boss. Leave your figures alone, smash the blasted scales ... now's the time you're going to save or to lose your soul."

What is it that people as disparate as Special Olympics boy, the Broadway hoofer, and the magnificently vital old Greek peasant have in common? Did we ever have it? Can we get it? Would we *want* it?

WHAT IS PASSION?

Fervent passion—the fire in the heart—is something so important to us that it becomes an insistent inner call, a flame that brightens our lives with light and warmth. At its purest and most glowing, it can be a torch to inspire and lead us or a campfire to comfort and rejuvenate us.

The operational definition for the purposes of this book contains two variations of passion:

---

1) *The excitement, ardor, and whole-heartedness that accompany a powerful emotional investment in an idea, cause, creative expression, or relationship;*

2) *A joyful zest for life, a way of being that celebrates one's experience.*

The first version is *focused passion*—passion <u>for and about something or someone.</u> An otherwise subdued person will take on a new energy when involved in, or even talking about, the object of his or her Passion.

The second version of passion is what the French call *joie de vivre* —the joy of living, a <u>way of being</u> not specific to an object or circumstance. Our friend Zorba epitomizes it. So does Auntie Mame, the glowing character from the book by Patrick Dennis. Her motto is:

21

LIFE IS A BANQUET!

and she grieves that so many people get stuck in one course and never sample others—or worse, that they let their spirits starve, malnourished for life.

THE QUEST FOR FIRE

Mihaly Csikszentmihalyi writes, "A joyful life is an individual creation that cannot be copied from a recipe."

People like Zorba and Mame celebrate life with a boisterous fervor that can be contagious. We become inspired and energized by their life passion. They are charismatic, inspiring, and occasionally exhausting to others.

Such hearty *joie de vivre* can make some onlookers nervous. There is something—well, primitive about it, like The Black Stallion.

Not all of us want to burn like the tiger in the night, except perhaps for brief bursts. Some people have a gentler version of *joie de vivre,* a mellow, deep appreciation for life. Theirs is a calm delight, more a sparkler than fireworks, more a candle than a torch.

Regardless of intensity, people of passion listen to their own drummer and dance to their internal rhythms. They don't require that others dance too, but they want respect for their right to their own dance.

LET YOUR LITTLE LIGHT SHINE!

We celebrate the fact that you are the architect of your own life. Your own style will shape your passion.

This book is dedicated to helping you ignite or reignite the fire in <u>your</u> heart that is the center of Soul. It can enable you to celebrate life more fully and joyously. It can lead you to express your highest good and deepest loves, and perhaps even go beyond the personal to the common welfare.

Even when you are only brightening the little corner of the world that is You, you are shining in a way that encourages other people to shine too.

CHAPTER 3

WHERE DOES PASSION COME FROM?

PASSION AS FEELINGS

Where do the powerful feelings come from that create passion in us? Their source has been debated for eons.

Maybe they come from our soul, the secret places of our hearts.

They undeniably have a chemical component. Certain medications can suppress or elevate a person's availability for passionate response.

Certainly they are strongly influenced by programming from parental influences, both behavioral and genetic.

Probably they are a complex mix of all these sources plus others we cannot now even imagine.

THE DNA CONNECTION

Your cousin Sam may have some of the same gestures as his grandfather, who died before Sam was born. Perhaps Sam even raises that left eyebrow the way Grandpa did. There can be only one explanation—we do possess **certain inborn gifts and traits**, including the way we're wired up neurologically. These traits affect not only mannerisms but even how we perceive and process information.

All people seem to be born with the capacity for passion unless they have very damaged brain chemistry. Such passion potential and its fulfillment are everyone's intrinsic birthright.

THE MODEL OF THE WORLD

The greatest determining factor in whether that passion will thrive or decline is *experience,* from which we built our expectations, values, self-perception—in short, our "model of the world."

> Our model of the world shapes how passionate we are, and how we are passionate.

As with all core perceptions and beliefs, we learn early whether, and when, passion is acceptable or unacceptable.

The family resides within the neighborhood, which in turn is a sub-culture of the social community. Authority figures—parents, grandparents, spiritual leaders, teachers—have enormous impact on us. The attitudes of our peers also affect us greatly; it takes a brave child to foster passion in the face of scorn from schoolmates. Still, if he is encouraged at home to be his own person and trust his own insides, he'll make it with his passion intact.

Even the most well-meaning families manage to give us both empowering and discouraging scripts about life choices.

HEALTHY PASSION

Healthy passion occurs when a person is encouraged to be authentic—to be one's real self, not a compliant or adapted clone.

What are messages families can send their children that will respect and even encourage their passion?

> *What do you think?*
> *Go for it!*
> *That was wonderful!*
> *How do you feel?*
> *Show off a little!*
> *Listen to your heart.*
> *We respect differentness.*
> *Sure you can!*

Explore, try new stuff.
You'll find a way.
You can do anything.
You're special
You're so smart!

Families and systems which communicate such messages believe that the purpose of parenting is to protect, nurture, and teach children while encouraging them to **unfold as themselves**, not little replicas of the authority figures.

Healthy passion also requires that the nurturing system teach the child when and how to express passion appropriately. We don't mean "appropriate" as in "be quiet and invisible," but in taking responsibility for your actions and their consequences. A child who has been *respected* and *directed* will learn appropriateness without squelching his spirit.

THE PATHS THAT LEAD TO PASSION

When you are fortunate enough to have heard these messages as a child, your energies are freed to claim your passion. Instead of depleting your vitality through anxiety, protective indifference, denial, avoidance, or compulsivity, you develop a dynamic sense of Self—self-respect, self-esteem, and healthy self-concept.

Where Does Passion Come From?

Healthy Passion Results

- **HONORING YOURSELF**—Because you have been honored and respected by others, you have genuine self-respect.

- **AUTHENTIC POWER**—Because you have learned to be accountable for your own happiness and the outcome of your actions, you can self-start and self-affirm.

- **EXPANDED COMFORT ZONE**—You dare more, risk more, because you carry your safety within you and know there is no such thing as failure, only learning.

- **FOLLOWING YOUR BLISS**—You trust and commit to those attitudes or endeavors that thrill or deeply satisfy you.

- **AFFIRMING THE *YES!* TO LIFE**—You respond with delight to most aspects of life, and can take pleasure in even its small events.

- **TRUSTING YOUR INNER CLICK**—You have learned your inner rhythms and can respond when the moment comes that says, "Now. Now is the time."

- **UNITING YOUR HEAD AND HEART**—You take charge of your inner dialogues and choices, and you use your brain to set those priorities that leave room and energy for your passions.

UNCONTROLLED PASSION

Clearly, we advocate cultivating healthy passion as part of affirmative, joyous living. On the other hand, unhealthy and uncontrolled behaviors, sometimes referred to as addictions, lead to emotional chaos.

Although many people use compulsive behaviors to numb their feelings, there are others who overindulge in alcohol, drugs, unhealthy eating, overwork, or obsession with a destructive relationship in order to achieve what seems to be a more passionate state of experience. Ultimately they may realize they've caught the smoke but missed the fire, chasing the wrong stuff to feel honest passion. By that time, however, they have become adrenalin junkies, hooked on the temporary excitement of an emotional or chemical high and requiring the next one, and the next.

There are people who overwork or overgive in order to feel acceptable, worthy to have earned their place in the world. Some use alcohol or chemicals to loosen their inhibitions so they can become aware of their feelings, or able to express them.

The result is the same: a coping mechanism that gets out of control and ends up using the user.

DARK PASSION

Uncontrolled negative feelings such as unreasoning jealousy, white-hot rage, overwhelming hatred, can release the darkest side of mankind's character. The so-called crime of passion is not only the momentary blindness of a cuckolded lover, it can be expressed in the desecration of a church or synagogue, the looting mob, the drive-by shooting.

These dark passions arise from our personal and collective pain or perceived powerlessness. They are there, ready to be unleashed in some form or another, in each of us. Until we acknowledge the dark side of human nature, including our own, we are not free to purposefully choose the healthy, enlightened side.

RECONCILING AND HEALING

The challenge for us all is how to take the energy that is inherent in a passionate response and focus it in a healthy way, for other peoples' sake but most especially for our own. *A dark or uncontrolled passion has its own perpetrator as an ultimate victim.*

THE UNCLAIMED PASSIONS

The intensity of our passions can make us feel so vulnerable that we may try to deny their power in our lives. This is true for life-affirming passions such as love, joy, and awe, as well as the more painful ones of rage, despair, guilt, and fear.

Dr. Georgia Witkins' research for her book Passions turned up the fact that both men and women fall into the habit of hiding feelings they decide are inappropriate. The most-often hidden emotions were fear and jealousy, with despair close behind. Other negative emotions trailed at a distance.

She also discovered that many people have enormous passions locked in their heart and cannot find or express them. These people cut themselves off from their emotions so totally that they simply are not aware of feeling them. The most frequently reported emotions that people said they never feel were infatuation and despair. Almost as many said they feel no rage or contentment in their lives.

Dr. Witkins says, "No rule says every person must feel every emotion, but can our lives [really] be so static that we never experience infatuation, despair, rage, or blissful contentment?"

Psychologists know that denial can exist to conceal its opposite feeling. The underlying emotion is so frightening or confusing that we deny its existence. Denial is an attempt to push the emotion back into Pandora's box.

Interestingly, no one in Dr. Witkins' study denied feeling anger, and almost no one denied feeling guilt, joy, or love. These are the emotions we speak of easily. These are the emotions of daily life.

STRETCHING YOUR PASSION PERIMETERS

All of us have passion limits. We have a familiar emotional range from Dispassionate to Overpassionate, and we have a home base, a comfort zone in which we feel safe.

A highly extroverted person may often be in a state of emotional intensity and activity. She has passionate interactions with others, full of emotionality from very high to very low, and she is comfortable with them.

Another may lead a life of quiet passion focused on his personal projects, from the computer to the loving restoration of his antique car. He does not display overt emotional expression.

The dramatic extrovert and serene introvert have something in common—both like to operate in their own familiar range of comfort. When they get out of that range, they can become uneasy, even anxious.

Unfamiliar emotions can make us feel more intensely than is customary for us. Some people say they feel overwhelmed when a passion knocks them into a new emotional range. That is the staggering experience of falling in love, or the heart-gripping sense of loss when someone dies or leaves us.

Any time we experience a change in our normal range of feeling, we have stretched our perimeters of passion. If we can withstand the energy change, we can develop a fuller and more complete emotional range.

The feelings that we call passions can be peak experiences that grab hold of us and sweep us into currents that redirect the stream of our lives. They can even inspire a new vision of the possible.

HOW DOES THE LIGHT GO OUT?

Part hereditary constitution, part chemical, largely learned through example and family values—passion gets its warmth and light from many sources.

In the next chapter we'll look at what happens to diminish passion. Before we can keep the light turned on, we have to determine what forces have been turning it off.

CHAPTER 4

HOW DO WE LOSE PASSION?

T. Berry Brazelton, the kind and venerable expert on child development and behavior, has said he can tell by the time a baby is nine months old whether or not the child has given up on life. *Nine months.*

That seemed impossible when we first heard it. All it takes is a visit to nursery of two-year-olds to see passion on the hoof! "Passion" in the dictionary should show a two-year-old. They shriek and roll on the floor and hug with great abandon—all their emotions right out there for the world to see, not yet censored.

That's what we thought. Then we heard other stories.

THE THROW-AWAY BABY

There is a woman we'll call Charlotte, with great beauty and lively intelligence. She is successful, personable, charming, witty, warm. She seems to have everything.

She says she believes she has never known a moment of passion in her whole life.

Charlotte was a third-generation unwanted, unwed pregnancy in a family of desperately poor immigrants whose religion forbade sex education and birth control. Her mother had to leave school before junior high to work for the money necessary for survival. When this teenager found out she was pregnant, she decided, as had several of the women in the family before her, to give the baby up for adoption. The only person in whom she confided was her older sister, who had also had to leave school. The sister said, "We can do it. We can somehow raise this child. Don't give it away." And she didn't.

The story goes that Charlotte was such a good baby. She was never any trouble. From the time she could sit up, they say, she would sit in her crib and literally twiddle her thumbs, spending silent hours not being any trouble.

She says, "I was somehow sure that I must not make any waves of any kind, ever, or I might be thrown away."

THE CONFORMITY DILEMMA

> *Most kids get socialized out of their passion!*

Again and again, either out loud or indirectly, children hear the admonitions: "Don't cry. Don't holler. Don't run. Don't squeal. Don't act or look different. Don't be seen or heard. Don't make waves. Don't rock the boat."

"You don't really feel what you feel, you feel what you're *supposed* to feel—and we will tell you what you're supposed to feel."

Some kids manage to keep their passion till they enter school, but passion is not encouraged by most school systems.

We talked to a Montessori teacher who knows a great deal about children. She has taught all ages for twenty years. We asked her, "When do the children start to repress their passion?"

She answered, "Let's see. It depends, of course, on their environment at home, as well as what teacher they have. In general, though, I'd say most kids start to lose it before they're three."

THE FARM IN THE STORM

There was a couple with three children who, when moving to a new city, chose to buy a house they could barely afford because it was in the "best" school system, and education was a high value to them.

The first week of school, their small daughter came home dejected and depressed. She didn't really want to talk about it, but they finally learned what had happened.

During art period the teacher said, "Children, today I want you to make a picture of a farm in a rainstorm." The kids all pulled out paints and paper and got started. All over the room were similar paintings—block-like barn, haystacks, some loopy flowers, a picket fence, some creatures that might have been cows or horses, a few chickens. There were jagged drawings of lightning and darkly scribbled rainclouds.

Except for this child's painting.

She gooshed her fingers around in the paint and <u>literally</u> painted up a storm. There were swirls of dark and light, streaks of blackened green, tree-shapes bent over from the wind.

And the teacher, after looking at her picture, had shown her the other children's efforts and then said she had to do hers over till she got it *right*.

An artist friend got tears in his eyes when he heard that story. He said, "Oh, what I would give to have back that primal emotion in my work. It breaks my heart even to hear that kids take 'art classes' and get shown how to 'do it right.' They can always learn perspective and composition later, but now they've got what a professional artist would give anything for. They can still <u>see</u>."

Our kids face that sort of drenching every day from a society that, for the most part, requires conformity. We may be a society that promotes rugged individualism in our adults, but we punish it in children, especially in school.

Fortunately for that little girl, she had parents who validated her interpretation of the storm. They told her it was just as good as, and possibly more interesting than, other people's versions. But how many parents would have taken the line that whatever the teacher says must be "right" because teachers are part of the Authority.

BIG BROTHER IS WATCHING

In his book <u>1984</u> George Orwell wrote of a society in which everyone was taken care of, no decisions to make, no thoughts to think, no opinions to have. Cradle-to-grave security. No risk—unless you gave the slightest hint of rebelling or even questioning Big Brother. History was rewritten, people's names and histories erased, any time it was necessary to realign facts to fit the party line.

Many people assumed Orwell was writing about communism. Actually, he was describing the programmed, systematic extinguishing of individual thought and volition that can happen under any system in which there must be only one Right, with everything else as Wrong.

Madelyn L'Engle's science fiction/fantasy <u>A Wrinkle in Time</u> is the tale of three children who must save the universe from a dark force which has already enveloped several planets. They are aided by three weirdly funny and wise old women, whose power can transport them across time and the cosmos but is not as strong as the intuition and courage and clear-sightedness of the children.

On a faraway planet, in a pretty town of pretty streets with absolutely identical houses, they encounter the dark force. The children who live there are all bouncing balls on the sidewalk—in perfect unison, with impassive faces and lusterless eyes—except one little boy, who is bouncing his ball to his own internal rhythm. His horrified mother darts out, scoops him up, and rushes back into the house, slamming the door. When our children knock, the mother opens the door a crack and anxiously assures them that her little boy is actually perfectly adapted, it won't be necessary to have him reprogrammed.

Here are some of the assumptions, rules, and direct or implied messages that throw cold water on the eager passion of children. You may know others.

Anti-Passion Devices

Don't talk back!
Look out. Be careful.
You made a fool of yourself (us).
You shouldn't feel that way.
Don't attract attention.
You can't get there from here.
Make up your mind!
You'll never have enough   (money)
(time)
(education)
(of what it takes).

They are versions of these major admonitions:

> *You don't count, aren't important.*
> *Individuality is an embarrassment.*
> *Don't take risks—life is dangerous.*
> *Your job is to please others.*
> *You don't have what it takes.*
> *You ought to be ashamed.*

In families, businesses and societies which require traditional conformity, passion is unseemly. Let's face it, passion, even resolute individuality, makes a lot of people anxious. To the authorities of the system it may appear to be lack of respect, or even rebellion, and must be quashed.

HYPERNICENESS

Author/poet Robert Bly writes in A Little Book on the Human Shadow—

> *We came as infants "trailing clouds of glory," arriving from the farthest reaches of the universe, bringing with us appetites well preserved from our mammal inheritance, spontaneities wonderfully preserved from our 150,000 years of tree life, angers well preserved from our 5,000 years of tribal life—in short, with our 360 degree radiance—and we offered this gift to our parents. They didn't want it. They wanted a nice girl or a nice boy.*

In trying to become the person we believe our parents really wanted, eventually we can lose connection with the true inner self.

Though often thought of as the domain of women (a nice girl is a <u>sweet</u> girl), many men struggle with the same "be nice" handicap. The program is based on your childhood perception (often accurate) that you won't get the approval of your caretakers if you have "negative" (not-nice) feelings or attitudes.

In such a family, everyone smiles and smiles and no one ever seems to get angry. Conflict resolution, of course, cannot occur. What conflict? Everyone is so agreeable, so nice. It's not real. To be real you must allow all feelings, even negative ones.

This is not to suggest that it is better to be abrasive, self-centered, and obnoxious. However, you run the risk of becoming a long-suffering victim if you habitually avoid telling the truth, even to yourself, because you don't want to make waves.

Ironically, to the degree you deny your disagreement or anger, you suppress your capacity for loving passion. Passion anesthesia is not selective—you can't cut off one feeling without diminishing all your feelings. What you can do is acknowledge the anger and then either release it or act on it constructively.

HIDING IN YOUR HEAD

There is another way to get cut off from your passions, and that's by making a fortress of your intellect. It is a process that John Bradshaw, well-known lecturer and author on recovery from addictions, calls "being cognitively dependent."

> *Such a [cognitively dependent] family tends to look very good on the outside. Family members appear to be sound thinking, wise, and reasonable. But when one examines the family dynamics, it becomes clear that a whole range of human needs is not being expressed and certainly not being negotiated. Matters may be discussed rationally, but feelings are never dealt with.*

... It's often difficult for a person who resides in a castle of logic and reason to realize that such a castle of the intellect may also have a dungeon.

In such an environment, you may have to justify your feelings as if proving up a case in a court of law. Parents or spouses may take the position, "If you can't persuade me that I would have identical feelings under similar circumstances, I won't accept your feelings as valid."

What child hasn't said, "When I grow up, I'm not gonna treat my kid like that!" Twenty years later, he's sounding just like his Dad, or she like her Mom.

When feelings are consistently discounted, derided, or suppressed—or just plain ignored—there is a dispiriting result that can haunt us for decades.

Anti-Passion Results

Sense of "Not Enough Time"—Compulsivity, tension, anxiety. The eternal hurry-up, endless to-do list, no time for Self.

Emptiness—lack of purpose; apathy, boredom, ennui; What's the point? or It's not worth the trouble.

External Motivation—No solid sense of Self. Mistrust of one's own internal barometer. Need for other people's approval or compliant behavior. Defining oneself through "helping" or by being cared for by others.

Isolation—Inability to connect to other people with a sense of security and intimacy.

Depression/Despair—Resignation; no connection to a sense of joy or even hopefulness.

Anxiety/Fear—Avoidance of the unfamiliar; unwillingness to risk; no inner safety, no urge to *go for it*.

Before we can change our programs and get back to the basic *Yes!* we were born with, we have to realize that our own Anti-Passion Devices are still humming away, probably just out of our conscious awareness.

If you really stop and think about it objectively, you'll realize what yours are. They are very familiar; you just don't often let them come into your conscious awareness. Take a moment to write them down as they occur to you. They can be a psychological roadmap for helping you see where you've gotten off the path you want.

BE PRO-PASSION!

Since you're reading this book, you must be interested in becoming Pro-Passion. In the next chapters we will look at some of the ways of passion—the various manifestations and styles of it, and how you can find it for yourself.

Be attuned to ideas that resonate within you. You may find that you're already a more passionate person than you'd realized, or you may discover a version of passion that really hums to you and that you'd like to cultivate.

Just remember this: since you are the person who is responsible for your outcome, you have to be the one who makes the choices. Although other people can and will make suggestion, requests, or demands, or give you well-meant instructions ...

> *Nobody but you has the right*
> *to choreograph your life!*

CHAPTER 5

FOCUSED PASSION: TO DO

It is a warm, still night. The stars shimmer and dance their ancient, familiar, cosmic choreography.

Steve is in love with stars. He decided a couple of years ago that instead of feeling unrequited love, he would do something about that passion. He studied videos of Carl Sagan's <u>Cosmos</u> series, finding something new and magical in each viewing. He bought a second-hand telescope, took a night course in astronomy, and pored over star charts until they were no more intimidating than street maps. On clear nights he spends hours among the stars. He likes to get lost in the stars and then gently bring himself back to earth.

Steve knows this particular passion might eventually fade. He has had other passions that glowed brightly for a while and then diminished, and he feels fine about that. While he remains starstruck, however, he intends to go on actualizing his passion by doing something with and about it.

BLAZING PASSION

Vincent Van Gogh burned with passion for painting. The pictures in his Starry Night series are filled with stars that are exploding worlds of passion. His sunflowers are aflame with yellow light.

If there is such a thing as passion incarnate, it can be found in those burning pictures. Would we want to be Van Gogh, to burn with such an inescapable flame? Perhaps not, but what a gift his life has been to the generations beyond him.

THE CONCEPT OF "FLOW"

Mihaly Csikszentmihalyi's book <u>Flow: The Psychology of Optimal Experience</u> is the result of more than twenty years' research on what he calls "flow"—a state of concentration so focused that it amounts to complete absorption in an activity. Flow comes when a person's body or mind is stretched to its limits in a voluntary effort to accomplish something difficult and worthwhile. These periods of concerted effort to master complex tasks and stretch our abilities can become the most satisfying and memorable in our lives. By pushing our boundaries we become more complex, passionate human beings.

Describing the lives of people who have focused their passion into flow, he writes:

> *Such individuals lead vigorous lives, are open to a variety of experiences, keep on learning until the day they die, and have strong ties and commitments to other people and to the environment in which they live.*

They enjoy whatever they do, even if tedious or difficult, they are hardly ever bored, and they can take in stride anything that comes their way. They are in control of their consciousness and lives.

These people are absorbed in something in which they find great fulfillment. This condition he calls "flow" is the state in which they are so deeply involved in an activity that they will do it even at great cost for the sake of the experience. The deep exhiliration and enjoyment they feel becomes chiseled on their memory. The dancer, teacher, baseball player, actor, social activist, all know about flow, and so can any of us when we are compellingly involved in our own experience of something we feel passionate about.

Csikszentmihalyi describes the essential aspects of this state of "flow."

Voluntary stretching

Focused passion often results in a person's body or mind stretched to its limits in an effort to accomplish something difficult and worthwhile. These periods of struggling to master complex tasks can result in expanded boundaries. By pushing yourself beyond your familiar comfort zone, you become a more complex, passionate being.

Present-centeredness

Most of us have had times of deep involvement in active sports, engaging conversations, an exciting career, or an intimate moment. The feeling is, "I never want this to end. This is as good as it gets!"

You are totally present at that moment, in a wholly contained bubble of existence. Time seems suspended—hours can go by and you never notice. One woman says, "When I'm absorbed and excited about what I'm writing, I can be on a long airplane ride and feel magically transported in only minutes to my destination."

Devoted commitment

Observe the Olympic hopeful in figure-skating training. She goes to the rink before dawn and again after school and practices until dinnertime. She passes up all other after-school activities, even the social ones. She has an iron determination to seize the moment—*carpe diem,* sieze the day!—because she knows her chance is <u>now</u>.

She is willing to forego the immediate gratification for the longer-term goal. If you talk with her in ten years, she will probably tell you she has never regretted the sacrifices she made, whether she won a medal or not.

An attitude of choice

To protect your passion and keep it focused, you must choose to be in charge of your inner dialogues and attitudes. That means using your good old intellect, your rational mind, to set the priorities and make the choices necessary to protect and liberate your passion.

It also means figuring out how to make it happen for yourself.

BECAUSE!

Nowhere is passionate commitment more evident than in service to an idea or cause. Environmental concerns, pro-choice vs. anti-abortion, save-this-landmark historic preservation, all are about a passionate resolve and highly personal emotional investment.

After Hitler had gobbled up his European neighbors, he fixed his sights on England. He was confident he would break the English people's spirit in a few days by systematically destroying their beloved London with his new secret weapon, the rocket-propelled buzzbomb.

Day and night his airborne blitzkrieg rained death on London. Its people learned to listen not just for the sound of the bomb's engine, but for the even more terrifying silence that meant it had begun its lethal descent.

After each bomb had done its worst, the Londoners put out what fires they could, shoveled debris, tended their wounded and buried their dead. And they never broke.

Churchill helped them stay resolute with these moving words:

We shall not flag or fail. ... We shall defend our island, whatever the cost may be. We shall fight on the beaches, we shall fight on the landing grounds, we shall fight in the fields and in the streets, we shall fight in the hills. We shall never surrender.

THE LASER EFFECT

When we focus our energy on something to which we are passionately committed, our passion can give it life.

The focused passion and resolve of the English people was like the laser that transforms ordinary light into an extraordinary force by concentrating its beam. Ordinary people, like ordinary light, can become transcended.

THE WALKING MEMORY BANK

When Charles Plumb's plane was shot down over Viet Nam, he parachuted safely to earth but was captured by the Viet Cong and imprisoned in the tiny, solitary cell where he was to spend the next seven years.

One day a thin wire was pushed under the wall of his cell. For several weeks he just watched it suspiciously. Eventually he learned that its movements transmitted a code which the prisoners had painstakingly devised to communicate with each other.

Charles learned that the prison held 147 fighter pilots and one Navy midshipman who had been captured after falling off his ship while on maneuvers. This sailor had memorized the name, rank, serial number, home town, and next of kin of every one of the 147 pilots. He knew he'd be one of the first prisoners released, because of his lower rank.

A year and a half later he was freed. After visiting his own family, he got on a bus and went to the home towns of every one of those 147 prisoners and told each family about its pilot.

Thus it was that when Charles Plumb was repatriated after seven long years, his father knew to expect him.

PLUMB'S PARACHUTE

After his return home, Charles set about rebuilding his life. He wrote a book, traveled, and told his story to the media.

One day he was finishing his meal in a restaurant when a man walked up to him and said,

"Are you Charles Plumb, the Navy pilot?"

"Yes, I am."

"Are you the Charles Plumb who spent seven years in a Viet Cong prison?"

"Yes, I am."

"I see your parachute worked. I packed it."

The packer of the parachute was so invested in the safety of the American pilots who would wear his chutes that he noted all their names and tracked their safety.

Charles Plumb was the recipient of two men's passionate commitment—one to reassure his family, the other to save his life—although neither man had ever met him.

NANCY BRINKER'S PASSION TO SAVE LIVES

Anyone who has ever watched a loved one struggle with a terrible terminal illness can understand Nancy Brinker's heartbreak as her sister, Suzy Komen, fought a three-year losing battle with breast cancer. Near the end, as Nancy held her after a particularly wracking bout with radiation-induced nausea, Suzy wept and said, "Nancy, you've got to do something to help other women. You have to find a way to speed up the research into this awful disease."

Nancy vowed to herself that she would do just that.

In October of 1982 the Susan G. Komen Foundation was officially launched, with Nancy Brinker as its passionate leader. Her staunchest supporter was husband Norman Brinker, who knew first-hand what she had gone through—his first wife, tennis champion Maureen "Little Mo" Connolly, died of ovarian cancer at age 34.

Although Nancy was reluctant to ask any of their friends for money, Norm thought they'd want to be involved, and the next day he started calling. Everyone contributed money, and even more important, extended their time and influence to get the word to nationally known people whose support would gain widespread recognition for the new foundation.

One friend called former first lady Betty Ford, who understood exactly what was at stake—she herself is a survivor of breast cancer. She agreed to attend the first fund-raising luncheon and now presents yearly the foundation award named for her, to honor someone who has promoted an awareness of breast cancer.

Eight years after she started the Foundation, Nancy Brinker was herself diagnosed with breast cancer. She believes that all her inquiry into the nature and treatment of breast cancer, on behalf of the Foundation, equipped her to make the tough choices she had ahead. Believing that Suzy died because her early treatment was non-aggressive, Nancy sought the expert oncologists at M.D. Anderson Cancer Center in Houston, where she chose to undergo the most aggressive treatments available. Suzy had died at 36. Nancy, at 37, survived the disease and has remained cancer-free for eight years.

Nancy Brinker is a woman obsessed, but it's a magnificent obsession. One of her most successful projects is the "Race for the Cure," a five-kilometer run and walk to raise money for cancer research. The Race is run in forty-eight cities and features catagories for wheelchair racers and children, as well as able-bodied men and women. It gives them all a chance, like Nancy, to *do something* to make a difference in their own communities. Three-quarters of the funds raised are kept in the cities where the races are held, to help deliver services to patients in that city.

In her passion to honor the promise made to her dying sister, Nancy Brinker has saved many lives, including her own.

CAREER PASSION

There are people who have a "calling" to a career, and though not all callings are religious, some impassioned people can be said to have a religious conviction.

Mary Kay Ash, for example.

During the Depression young Mary Kay started off selling brushes and household cleaners through Stanley Home Products. She then joined another company as head of its sales training. After eleven years, she came to work one day to discover that the male assistant she'd been training for almost a year had just been made her boss, at twice her salary.

When she protested this injustice to her superiors, she was ignored. The business policy was covert but clear: if you were female, you were supposed to be part of the support system, not management. Mary Kay quit her job.

That's when her passion was born. She made a decision which later became a credo: she would create a sales business in which women would be treated respectfully and their self-esteem fostered. Unlike traditional organizations with quotas and caps on income, there would be no ceiling on the amount of money a representative could make.

She invested her life savings of $5,000 to start her new company. A month later her husband collapsed at the breakfast table and died of a heart attack. With children to support and a fledgling business, she plowed ahead.

In stark contrast to the attitudes of the company she had quit, Mary Kay Ash made the Golden Rule her major mission statement. A sincerely religious woman, she has consistently urged to members of the Mary Kay enterprise that they put God and their families before their careers.

Because of her vision, thousands of women have become moderately to wildly successful in the Mary Kay business. Sales have risen from $198,000 in 1963 to over $613,000,000 today. There are 6,500 beauty consultants and sales directors driving complimentary automobiles and at least seventy women who have earned commissions of a million dollars or more.

To visit a Mary Kay convention is to be in the midst of passion. Of course there is the usual conviviality and enthusiasm expected at such a sales celebration, but there is also a mentoring atmosphere among women devoted to developing each other's leadership potential.

Their excitement is understandable. Women with no business experience and little education, as well as restless professionals, have found an entrepeneurial opportunity in which they'll not only be able to make good incomes, they will be appreciated and supported all along the way. One woman says, "Mary Kay calls you her daughter and looks you dead in the eye. She makes you feel you can do anything. She's sincerely concerned about your welfare."

Mary Kay's big heart has not only enriched her consultants, it has paid off for her as well. The Ash family fortune is estimted at $320 million—from an initial investment of $5,000.

It was born of a passionate commitment to creating a business environment in which women would be respected, not exploited or patronized.

LORENZO'S OIL

The searing film Lorenzo's Oil tells the true story of the Odone family and their passionate fight to save their son's life. Their little boy Lorenzo was diagnosed with ALD, a progressive neurological disease that attacks only healthy male children and over a two-year period takes first their neurology and then their lives.

The Odones fervently immersed themselves into learning everything they could about biochemistry, neurology, and human anatomy. Some parents of other ALD patients chided them, saying, "How could you try to prolong Lorenzo's life? Look how he suffers. You are being selfish to hang on to him."

Lorenzo's parents had quite another view. They were fighting against time, the most implacable enemy, and they were fighting not only for Lorenzo's life but also for the lives of all the other little boys who would be afflicted in the future. Although the neurological damage caused by ALD is irreversible, they hoped to discover a way to halt the symptoms—a way to arrest the disease in its very early stages, to put it on Hold.

Much of the medical establishment was either patronizing or hostile to the Odones, sometimes actually blocking their efforts. The parents were having to do battle on many fronts, and meantime their little boy was slipping down and away from them.

Through a mighty and obsessive will, and fueled by rage at the cruel illness as well as passionate love for their son, the Odones became more knowledgeable about the disease than all but a handful of people in the world. Eventually they created a breakthrough in medical research that lengthened the life of their son. He is still alive at fourteen, the first child to have lived longer than two years after initial diagnosis.

Their passion on behalf of Lorenzo and all the other little boys has had a result that is even more moving.

*There are hundreds of cases
of arrested ALD, right now,
all around the world.*

The stargazer. Vincent Van Gogh. The Olympic hopeful. The beseiged people of London. The midshipman and the parachute packer. Nancy Brinker. Mary Kay Ash. Lorenzo Odone's mother and father. What do these people have in common?

They used the steps of focused passion to <u>actualize</u> what mattered to them. They struggled and stretched their limits in service to their dreams, beliefs, what they deeply care about. They entered the present-centeredness that is called "be here now." They kept a purposefulness that informs their actions, and they maintained a disciplined attitude to keep themselves focused.

WHAT ABOUT YOU?

Most of us are ordinary people, really. We lead fairly mundane lives and are usually pretty content with them. The most fortunate of us, however, are those who have some area of life in which we focus our passion and <u>do</u> something with it.

THE FLYING BOOKKEEPER

There once was a timid bookkeeper whose secret desire was to become a commercial pilot. There were two problems: (1) she was barely making ends meet financially, and (2) she'd never even been up in a plane. And, of course, the biggest problem was that she had never given herself permission, much less commitment, to make her dream a reality.

Finally, she went to the local flight field and said to the instructor, "I want an introductory flight." After all, she didn't know for sure that she would even like flying. But of course she did, even more than she had imagined.

She offered her instructor an exchange of services. She would do his bookkeeping, keep track of maintenance schedules and flight records, pay bills, and prepare his tax returns. She proposed to work every Saturday for as many hours as these services required, in return for one hour a week of flight instruction and plane time. He agreed.

She took it one step at a time. She got her student license. She soloed. Passed the written test. Got her instrument rating. Did her cross-country. Got her pilot's license and certification in multi-engine and jet planes. It took her several years, but that was fine, because she was not only moving resolutely toward her goal, she was enjoying the process.

The last we heard, she was company pilot for a very successful medium-sized international corporation. She literally flies all over the world.

Joseph Campbell, the educator, spellbinding lecturer, and author of The Power of Myth, said passionately:

> **Follow your bliss!**

It doesn't matter what it is. It needn't be highflown or deeply significant for all mankind. Maybe it's a long-suppressed desire to learn ballroom dancing, to feel yourself float around a dance floor, swaying like a reed in the evening breeze. Maybe it's to become a speaker, or to develop a new hybrid rose, or to start horseback riding again.

Maybe, like us, it's to write a book about something you passionately believe in.

PASSION AS DOING

Passion as <u>doing</u> entails commitment for something, an idea or ideal, vocation or avocation, art or mission. Its energy is specific and laser-like, with a desired outcome. It is often intense, absorbing, in many ways inner-directed.

LIFE AS A LOVE AFFAIR

There is another kind of passion which is absorbing in a different way.

The French call it *joie de vivre*. It is the *passion of being* and is generalized to all of what novelist Dan Jenkins calls "life its ownself." In the next chapter we will look at passion as a way of life, a pervasive approach to this whole crazy, complicated business of being human.

CHAPTER 6

PASSION FOR LIFE: TO BE

THE LOVE AFFAIR WITH LIFE

The most fundamental principle of *joie de vivre* is this: Love is a spiritual resource within ourselves. This deep connection to life and spirit is the wellspring of lifelove.

Too often the culture points us with movies, songs, and love stories to the perception that love is only generated between people. This simply isn't so.

Your ability to love and connect fully is self-generated. It is by honoring your own authenticity, feelings, and inner knowing that true love can be generated—for yourself, for others, *for life*.

LIFELOVERS

Think of someone, real or imaginary, who sparkles with life, who seems to embrace the joy of being alive.

Katherine Hepburn springs to mind. She takes risks, speaks her mind, and inhabits the present fully. She laughs easily and loudly and glows with all of life's wondrous possibilties. She accepts other people's idiosyncracies, is tolerant of most things—except intolerance. She is never bored. She reaches out and grabs experience. At the age of 85 she still swims in the ocean regardless of the season—and ocean dips in New England winters are *invigorating.* (But then, that's what keeps her young: her vigor, her gusto.)

Kate Hepburn's being is ripe with the juice of life. Whatever her current situation, she makes the best of it and marches confidently on.

PASSION AS *YES!*

We believe that happiness is based on the passionate *Yes!* to life, with all its vicissitudes. As anyone who has been depressed knows, there is no happiness in giving up, saying No to life and withdrawing into isolation, where resignation and despair dwell.

Jay grew up on the mean streets of Philadelphia. By the time he was in his early twenties, every knuckle of his right hand was misshapen from having been broken in fights. He'd been in and out of jail for years. In prison he met someone who offered him another view of life, and he decided to try it out. It worked for him, and he ended up as a trainer in an agency whose purpose is to care for and rehabilitate juvenile offenders.

Jay's life view is one of quiet triumph. Still, he is a passionate man, absolutely committed to giving kids another chance. He shares with them his life motto:

> Whatever happens, I can handle it.
> And if I can't — I can handle that.

That's not resignation. That's acceptance. It's an essential for joie de vivre, because if you embrace life, you gotta embrace all of it. Hard times? You bet. It's part of being human. But there is still love and joy and beauty.

BECOMING YOURSELF

Carl Rogers wrote in his book <u>On Becoming a Person:</u>

Becoming a person means that the individual moves toward being, knowingly and acceptingly, the process which he inwardly and actually IS. He moves away from being what he is not, from being a facade.

He is not trying to be more than he is, with the attendant feelings of insecurity or bombastic defensiveness. He is not trying to be less than he is, with the attendant feelings of guilt or self-depreciation. He is increasingly listening to the deepest recesses of his psychological and emotional being, and finds himself increasingly willing to be, with greater accuracy and depth, that self which he most truly is.

PASSION IS IN THE PROCESS

The *joie de vivre* aspect of passion, <u>being in</u> passion as a way of life, arises from the ability to focus on the inner self and recognize—and then choose—what creates an inner sense of happiness and aliveness. It requires paying attention to the *process* of living.

Benjamin Huff, in his brilliant little book <u>The Tao of Pooh</u>, uses the characters from <u>Winnie the Pooh</u> to illustrate this way of being in the Now. Christopher Robin asks:

> *"What do you like doing best in the world, Pooh?*
> *"Well," said Pooh, "what I like best —" and then he had to stop and think. Because although Eating Honey <u>was</u> a very good thing to do, there was a moment just before you began to eat it which was better than when you were, but he didn't know what it was called.*

Benjamin Huff goes on to say:

> *The honey doesn't taste so good once it is being eaten; the goal doesn't mean so much once it is reached; the reward is not so rewarding once it has been given. If we add up all the rewards in our lives, we won't have very much. But if we add up the spaces <u>between</u> the rewards, we'll come up with quite a bit. And if we add up the rewards <u>and</u> the spaces, then we'll have everything— every minute of the time that we spent.*

...That doesn't mean that the goals we have don't count. They do, mostly because they cause us to go through the process, and it's the <u>process</u> that makes us wise, happy, or whatever. If we do things in the wrong sort of way, it makes us miserable, angry, confused, and things like that. The goal has to be right for us, and it has to be beneficial, in order to ensure a beneficial process. But aside from that, it's really the process that's most important. <u>Enjoyment</u> of the process is the secret that erases the myths of the Great Reward and Saving Time.

STAYIN' ALIVE!

We all know people who aren't truly alive. They walk and talk, but they're like sleepwalkers, never really awake.

It doesn't have to be that way. We all have a choice to be awake, aware, alive, to notice and rejoice in the world around us.

Alice Walker's <u>The Color Purple</u> tells the story of a young woman who wakes not only to her own worth but to the beauty of a world in which she at last perceives her value. She says that God wants his handiwork to be noticed and celebrated, that people should never pass a field of purple—that wonderful color purple—without appreciating it.

In <u>Pilgrim at Tinker Creek</u>, the book for which she won a Pulitzer Prize, Annie Dillard writes about people who gained their sight after an entire lifetime of blindness. Some were frightened or overwhelmed by their new perceptions, and a few actually closed their eyes to return to familiar, safe blackness. Others were mesmerized by the world of sight.

> *Of a patient just after her bandages were removed, her doctor writes, "The first things to attract her attention were her own hands; she looked at them very closely, moved them repeatedly to and fro, bent and stretched the fingers, and seemed greatly astonished at the sight." One girl was eager to tell her blind friend that "men do not really look like trees at all," and was astounded to discover that her every visitor had an utterly different face.*
>
> *Finally, a twenty-two-year-old girl was dazzled by the world's brightness and kept her eyes shut for two weeks. When at the end of that time she opened her eyes again, ...the more she now directed her gaze about her, the more it could be seen how an expression of gratification and astonishment overspread her features; she repeatedly exclaimed: "Oh, God! How beautiful!"*

BEVERLY'S CELESTIAL ANIMALS

One of the most passionate, lyrical novels of this or any other century is Mark Helprin's <u>Winter's Tale.</u> One of its remarkable characters is Beverly Penn, a turn-of-the-century girl of nineteen who has tuberculosis and knows she will die, but is so enamored of life that each of her days has more vitality in it that many people's decades.

She spends her feverish nights on a rooftop platform, watching the sky. She quite literally hears and sees things in it that other people cannot.

She continued to speak in calm certainties. "There are animals in the stars...with a pelt of light and deep endless eyes. Astronomers think that the constellations were imagined. They were not imagined at all. There are animals, far distant, that move and thrash smoothly, and yet are entirely still. They aren't made up of the few stars in the constellations that represent them—they're too vast—but these point in the directions in which they lie."

"How can they be bigger than the distance between stars?" he asked.

"All the stars that you can see in the sky don't even make up the tip of a horn, or the lash of an eye. Their shaggy coats and rearing heads are formed of a curtain of stars, a haze, a cloud. The stars are a mist, like shining cloth, and can't be seen individually. The eyes of these creatures are wider than a thousand of the universes that we think we know. And the celestial animals move about, they frisk, they nuzzle, they paw and roll—all in infinite time, and the crackling of their coats is what makes the static and hissing which bathes an infinity of worlds."

Peter Lake stared at the water as it came over the fall. "I'm as crazy as you are," he said, "maybe crazier. I believe you. I do believe you."

"That's only love," Beverly answered. "You don't have to believe me. It's all right if you don't. The beauty of truth is that it need not be proclaimed or believed. It skips from soul to soul, changing form each time it touches, but it is what it is, and I have seen it, and someday you will, too."

Joie de vivre is, simply, the love of life. And why <u>not</u> joyfully celebrate it? Why not take care of and love yourself, and surround yourself with people, settings, and pursuits that give you energy and joy?

This is your *life* —the only one you'll get as the You that you know. Why not really <u>be</u> here for the whole show?

An old woman was asked how, with her stiffness and poor sight and trembly hands, she could be so exuberant about life. She grinned and answered, "Sure beats the alternative!"

In his little cult classic book, <u>Das Energi</u>, Paul Williams sums it up with these words:

> *Vote with your life.*
>
> *Vote Yes.*

CHAPTER 7

THE SEVEN PATHS TO PASSION

Each of the seven aspects of passion is a path back to the center of your most authentic Self. In the truest sense of the expression, they are the paths back to your heart.

They are not taken sequentially, because life doesn't work that way. We zig and zag and sometimes we backtrack, but ultimately, if we are purposeful and dedicated, we can get to our destination.

One person's destination is simply to be more fully alive, more awake and aware. A woman we know says, "I created this home over twenty years, and now I want to really appreciate every day I spend in it. It is a major contributor to the delight in my life. I nest and rest here when I need sanctuary, and I play and work here when I feel energetic. It is home base for me, and I don't want to take it for granted."

Another person's passion destination is concrete: to paint again, or to finally learn to fly a plane, or master a language, or gain custody of a neglected child, or finally get that GED.

The same seven paths apply to them all:

PATH #1:   Honoring Yourself
PATH #2:   Claiming Your Authentic Power
PATH #3:   Expanding Your Comfort Zone
PATH #4:   Following Your Bliss
PATH #5:   Affirming the YES! to Life
PATH #6:   Trusting the Inner Click
PATH #7:   Uniting Your Head and Heart

Following the seven paths will unite your conscious, purposeful will with an inner knowing of what is right for you. The paths will be your guide, pointing toward unforeseen meetings, inspired thoughts, and positive connections.

Though some of the terrain may seem unfamiliar, listen and feel for the echo of other times, earlier days when you knew all this consciously.

You know it still.

All that remains is for you to act on it.

These words from the German poet Goethe may help to light your journey:

Until one is committed there is hesitancy, the chance to draw back, always ineffectiveness. Concerning all acts of initiative and creation there is one elementary truth, the ignorance of which kills countless ideas and splendid plans: that the moment one definitely commits oneself, then Providence moves too.

All sorts of things occur that would never otherwise have occurred. A whole stream of events issues from the decision, raising in one's favor all manner of unforeseen incidents and meetings and material assistance which no one could have dreamt would have come his way.

Whatever you can do, or dream you can, begin it.

Boldness has genius, power, and magic in it.

Begin it now.

PATH #1

HONORING YOURSELF

*Your vision will become clear
only when you can look into your own heart.
Who looks outside, dreams;
who looks inside, awakes.*

— Carl Jung

Passion dwells in the Natural Child part of us all. Some people think it is the closest we get to the Divine. It is primary emotion, the core of the truest Self, and it needs to be looked after and protected.

There are two ways we look after a child. We **nurture** through cherishing and **protect** by setting limits. The same is true of our passion. Both kinds of caretaking require understanding and compassion for this most authentic Self, so we can know how to give it room to breathe, keep it from being smothered or made unimportant.

HONORING YOUR INNER VOICE

To be truly observant, you must sit back in your eyes and open your ears, ready to *notice* what's going on around you.

What about your own internal geography? Do you regularly stroll around inside yourself, tuned in to the messages you are sending yourself?

Do you write down your dreams, which are, after all, coded messages? Your unconscious self is leaving stories for your conscious waking self to decode.

MAGICAL PROPERTIES

There is a woman of our acquaintance who is given to weird and vivid dreams.

As a child she used to write short stories for her little sister, and later wrote adolescent science-fiction tales.

One of her adult dreams came to her like a story unfolding, a tiny sci-fi videoplay complete with title: *Magical Properties.* It came (that is, she told it to herself while asleep) in a time of great personal stress which to her mind meant impending growth. Although she didn't like the discomfort she was going through—hadn't asked for it, felt it was thrust on her—she sensed that she was changing for the better.

This is what she wrote to describe the dream:

THE DREAM, A STORY:

"Mind you don't get too close to that one," the curator said. "He's got magical properties, that one has. He's your Venusian Ear Frog. He'll jump in your ear and eat you all up from the inside out, tooth and toenail, hair and eyeteeth, then spit you back out and you never knew it happened. But they say you're never the same afterward.

"Nobody knows why he's adapted just to the ear— don't see why he couldn't choose the nostril or mouth, but the ear it is. There's even left-eared and right-eared Frogs, so they say. I've never seen him do it, myself, but the supplier that bagged him told me about it, and he turned pale as a bubble and crossed himself. Can't say I believe it all, but I'll tell you this much, _he_ sure did."

"But why does it do that?" the girl asked, shivering at the prospect.

"Curious fella," answered the curator.

Our storytelling friend says she felt detached within the dream, an observer who could still somehow feel the feelings.

I became all the parts, so that the dream was like a radio show. People marveled at my creativity, both as a writer and an actor. I felt very happy about that, validated, appreciated, relieved.

YOU ARE THE ONE WHO WALKS IN YOUR MOCCASINS

No one is qualified to decode your dreams except you, for the obvious reason that they are messages from your interior. A dream interpretation book can only tell you what other people project onto dreams similar to yours, their meanings.

If you have an idea of what *Magical Properties* "means," remember that your interpretation is a message you are sending to yourself.

The dreamer of *Magical Properties* laughs as she finds her meaning of the dream. She says,

> *It's not exactly subtle. The circumstances of my life right now are eating me up, but I know I will come out of them stronger and wiser. I learned a long time ago to trust my own creativity, even though when I'm in the soup I don't know how I'm going to get out.*
>
> *That's funny, that phrase "in the soup." Did you know that after a caterpillar spins his coccoon, he dissolves into a kind of soup? Breaks right down to his essential molecules, and then they rearrange into a new life form, the butterfly.*
>
> *I guess it's really okay to be in the soup!*

SAM'S DREAM

Sam dreamed that he was sitting at a large dinner table with his family, some friends, and some strangers. Great platters of food were being passed around, boardinghouse style. When the fried chicken platter came to him, he thought, "I mustn't take a good piece of chicken. I don't want to be a hog." And he took a scrawny wing.

Likewise, when the mashed potatoes came around, he took only a tiny dab. And so forth and so on, until his plate had five or six miniature scoops of food. Sam says, "It looked like I was dishing up a meal for a little elf." The platters continued to go round and round the table. They seemed always to be full, yet Sam never took more than a thimbleful on each passing.

When he woke up, he had a terrible feeling of isolation, wistfulness, loneliness, and sorrow. He felt profoundly undernourished.

Sam says his dream was a perfect parable to remind himself how he tends to get so busy taking care of other people and of *things* that he gets himself into a self-imposed servitude.

KEEPING THE BAROMETER INSIDE

When you were a child, you spake as a child, you understood as a child, and you learned to please as a child. Now that you are a grown-up, the barometer about how you're doing and who you are and what values you have belongs inside of you.

Ironically, you had it once, back in that childhood, before you got taught to shape yourself to others' expectations. Back when you trusted your mermaidhood.

THE LITTLE MERMAID

Robert Fulghum, in his delightful book <u>All I Really Need to Know I Learned in Kindergarten</u>, tells about trying to get a wired-up group of gradeschoolers to take part in a game of Giants, Wizards, and Dwarfs.

As the pandemonium reached critical mass, he yelled out to the kids that they had to decide <u>right now</u> which they would be—a GIANT, a WIZARD, or a DWARF. As the groups consulted, Fulghum felt a tug at his pants leg.

A small child stands there looking up, and asks in a small, concerned voice, "Where do the Mermaids stand?"

Where do the Mermaids stand?

A long pause. A very long pause. "Where do the Mermaids stand?" says I.

"Yes. You see, I am a Mermaid."

"There are no such things as Mermaids."

"Oh, yes, I am one!"

She did not relate to being a Giant, a Wizard, or a Dwarf. She knew her category. Mermaid. And was not about to leave the game and go over and stand against the wall where a loser would stand. She intended to participate, wherever Mermaids fit into the scheme of things. Without giving up dignity or identity. She took it for granted that there was a place for Mermaids and that I would know just where.

Well, where DO the Mermaids stand? All the "mermaids"—all those who are different, who do not fit the norm and who do not accept the available boxes and pigeonholes?

Answer that question and you can build a school, a nation, or a world on it.

What was my answer at the moment? Every once in a while I say the right thing. "The Mermaid stands right here by the King of the Sea!"

...It is not true that Mermaids do not exist. I know at least one personally. I have held her hand.

HONORING YOUR WANTS

We all want to be good guys. We don't want to be "selfish"—so in the name of graciousness we often put ourselves last, over and over again, until we're depleted. Then, ironically, we don't have anything for ourselves <u>or others</u>, and often become annoying, self-righteous martyrs in the process. And so nobody wins.

THE RIGHT TO SAY *NO*

Some of us have as a major criterion for friendship that the other person be someone who knows how to take care of himself. That way, if a friend says she will be glad to pick you up at the airport at 2:00 AM, you don't have to shuffle and scuff your toe and say, "Are you sure you don't mind? I really don't want to put you out. I really could take the shuttle bus. Are you <u>sure</u> you don't mind?" We've got the kind of friends who would answer, if asked such fatuous questions, "Hey, Ace, I wouldn't have offered if I minded. OK?"

It is wonderful not to have to feel responsible for looking after someone else's feelings, knowing instead that they are perfectly competent to take care of themselves.

Does this kind of friendship result in one or both people becoming arrogant or insensitive or tactless or mean-spirited? It certainly doesn't seem to. On the contrary, we nurture and spoil each other when we feel like doing that.

What we don't do is put out martyr energy.

An insightful woman once said, "If you can't tell me No, then your Yesses don't mean anything."

That doesn't mean we have to be rude or unfeeling. It does mean we have a right to tell the truth about ourselves, about what we're up to and what we're not.

Wherever possible, choose comrades and associates who are prepared to accept you as you are, warts and all.

WHEN I SAY *NO*, I FEEL—BETTER!

In an assertiveness class a woman we'll call Annie said, "But I don't know <u>how</u> to say No and have the other person still like me or not try to manipulate me into changing my mind."

One of her buddies said, "Hey, Annie, you know the definition of failure? Trying to please everybody."

Another one said, "I've always liked the phrase 'What is it about No that you don't understand?'"

That got a laugh, but it wasn't Annie's style—it didn't fit for her, made her feel like a smart-aleck. We finally role-played a scene in which she was being telephoned to be on yet another committee, and the caller was ruthlessly aggressive.

Here is how it finally came out.

Path #1: Honoring Yourself

Person playing Caller: But you've just got to do this! The whole project will go down the tubes without you. You're the only one who can save us.

(Observer: Boy, that's really dirty pool. The old emotional blackmail number.)

Annie: I really wish I could clone myself and have time to do this, but I've made myself a promise to only pledge 50% of myself to other people, and keep the other 50% for my family and myself. And I've already said Yes to all I can and still keep my word to myself.

PPC: (spontaneously) Boy, I wish I'd thought of that when they called me to be on this dadgum telephone committee!

THE TO-DO LIST THAT ATE NEW YORK

The plain fact is, the To-Do List never gets finished. By the time you've ticked off the bottom item, it's sprouting out the top again.

Of course there are some Shoulds and Oughts we have to live by. Besides the obvious ones that are called the law of the land, we have responsibilities. As Robert Frost said, "But I have promises to keep, and miles to go before I sleep, and miles to go before I sleep." It is honorable to keep your word, and besides, you don't want to let other people down.

But what about yourself? Do you take care of other people and obligations so thoroughly that you're letting <u>yourself</u> down?

You do get satisfaction from finishing the weeding or marking something else off your To-Do list. Are we actually suggesting that you consider postponing your chores in service to your passion?

Absolutely.

Honoring your passion requires that you become your own advocate, not just other people's. It is literally Self-respecting. If you don't, you may end up on your deathbed with a big imaginary leftover To-Do list staring you in the face, instead of the satisfaction of knowing you LIVED your life, didn't just react to everybody's expectations, or what you thought they were.

As Shakespeare said:

> *To thine own self be true.*
> *Thou canst not then be false to any man.*

PATH #2:

CLAIMING YOUR AUTHENTIC POWER

I think I can, I think I can, I think I can ...
I thought I could! I thought I could!
— <u>The Little Engine That Could</u>

EXTERNAL POWER

Traditionally, power has been defined by external events or by control over someone else.

Gary Zukav in his book <u>The Seat of the Soul</u> describes this concept of external power as the power to control the environment and those within it.

External power can be acquired or lost, as in the stock market or an election. It can be bought or stolen, transferred or inherited.

> *It is thought of as something that can be gotten from someone else, or somewhere else. One person's gain of external power is perceived as another person's loss.*
>
> *The result of seeing power as external is violence and destruction. All of our institutions—social, economic and political—reflect our understanding of power as external.*
>
> *Families, like cultures, are patriarchal or matriarchal. One person "wears the pants." Children learn this early, and it shapes their lives.*

External power assumes that we need others—other people, more money, degrees, titles, status, success—to validate us.

PERSONAL POWER

Personal power results when we transcend to the realization that we can self-validate.

Zukav writes:

> *Authentic power has its roots in the deepest source of our being. Authentic power cannot be bought, inherited, or hoarded. An authentically empowered person is incapable of making anyone or anything a victim.*
>
> *...When we align our thoughts, emotions, and actions with the highest part of ourselves, we are filled with enthusiasm, purpose, and meaning. Life is full and rich. We have no memory of fear. We are joyously and intimately engaged with our world.*

THE LOVE WITHIN

Those who declare that life or love has passed them by are mistakenly looking to someone or something outside themselves for love. As you begin developing love and self-respect from within, you no longer feel at the mercy of people, situations, and conditions. You become master of your world and are free (relatively) from hurt, fear, and disappointment. You feel balanced enough within yourself to effectively handle the fear and disappintments.

AM I OKAY?

Our society deeply conditions us to crave approval from other people.

As young children we begin the quest to make sense of the world and our place in it, and to discover who we are. That discovery always takes place in relation to other people. Interaction with others creates self-concept.

While children are still so malleable, there are always adults who believe that their job is to shape the child into who they think he ought to be—in some harsh instances, who he'd better be or suffer terrible consequences. Parents, teachers, all kinds of public institutions, truly and with the best intent see their role as potters shaping clay. Unusual textures in a child should be kneaded until they are smooth and conforming to society's idea of acceptable.

Of course we need to teach children the limits that make up a sense of personal ethics and respect for others, including socialization to our society's notion of civil behavior. Neglecting to instill those limits can result in a child who either doesn't have a clue about how to behave in society, or else sees himself as the King of the Universe, entitled to roll over others in the pursuit of what he wants.

CHILD RESPECT

Beyond establishing those healthy limits, however, it is possible to see child-caring in another way—a way that fosters self-validation.

This second view holds that adults can be guides and mentors, fostering and celebrating the uniqueness of the child, listening to his feelings and viewpoints, and more importantly, teaching him to do the same.

Actually, receiving respect is the <u>only</u> way he'll learn genuine respect for others—that is, to regard and honor others' world view as being perhaps different but legitimate.

Too often children are forced into obeying without their own feelings and viewpoints being considered or even allowed to be expressed. The message is, "You'll respect me, *or else.*"

If he is coerced into obeying without his feelings and viewpoints being heard or considered, what passes for respect is actually intimidation.

He will learn to obey authority and salute the uniform and will require that those under his control do the same, without ever knowing how, or even wanting, to understand another person's viewpoint.

The child grows up with a demeaning belief system that says:

Path #2: Claiming Your Authentic Power

- There is *only one* right way to do things.
- If you don't agree with it, *you're wrong.*
- I'm going to beat you down through disapproval, debate, or punishment until you bend to my way of thinking.

When a large or influential enough segment of society holds that value system, what results is a totalitarian state.

Sadly, many a household is a little totalitarian state, with no right to be heard at a fair trial and no appeal. In such an environment children grow up to see power as wholly external.

IT'S SCARY

With so much conditioning to accept external power, no wonder we keep hoping for an external environmental change that will finally make us acceptable and secure. We look outside ourselves for our validation and safety.

As friend Ann says, "So much of our culture says external power is the only kind, so you keep thinking *if only* —if only I can get more money, more status, become more accomplished, then I'll be safe. Then I'll be good enough."

> Authentic power is knowing that
> you are good enough right now

...and that the most important voice to heed is the one coming from your own Inner Wisdom. It is the sum of your values, ethics, knowledge, and feelings.

PLUGGING IN TO YOUR AUTHENTIC POWER

We know a family whose income was always stretched so thin you could read a newspaper through it. The parents hated to always be saying No when their kids wanted to do something that cost money, but they often had to. One day Mother organized the making of three lists:

Fun Things to Do That Are Free
   Fun Things to Do That Are Cheap
     Expensive Things Worth Saving For

The first two lists were stuck onto the refrigerator and added to constantly. Board games, hide-and-seek, sleep-overs, kite flying, crawdad fishing and exploring the creek, cook-outs, craft projects, camping trips, reading, writing stories, trips to the library, trying new recipes—these were only some of the activities that made it to the first two lists.

Somehow the third list never got off the ground. There were always too many day-to-day financial fires to put out. However, when the kids became old enough, they all got jobs after school (or before)—paper routes, working in a sandwich shop, waitressing in a pancake house. They helped to pay for the reliable but unglamorous used cars they eventually bought, and they earned the money to buy special clothes that the family's budget couldn't manage.

Although that family never was able to save for future needs, the kids grew up resourceful. Each in turn managed to manifest for himself or herself the things that mattered enough.

These young people had it hard in some ways, though certainly not as hard as most of the world. Although they were nurtured and appreciated greatly as children, they were forced by circumstance into adulthood faster than they would have liked, and sometimes they were resentful or overwhelmed or depressed at the magnitude of being financially responsible while still in their teens. Yet they were less deprived, in an ironic way, than the kids who have everything handed to them. Those are the ones who don't know how to be resilient and resourceful when life hands them a hardship.

HARRY TRUMAN'S LEGACY

When Franklin Delano Roosevelt died, he had been President for thirteen years. He had seen the country through a devastating depression. He had been at the helm through a horrendous war, which was drawing to a climax. He was a handsome, charismatic, cultured, charming man with immense social grace.

And then he suffered a cerebral hemorrhage and died, just like that.

World War II was ending in Europe, and now the country needed a forceful leader to deal with the Pacific war and to bring us to an end of the bloodshed and pain.

We got Harry Truman, a feisty little bantam rooster of a man, a no-nonsense salt-of-the-earth Midwesterner, appalling straightforward. What you saw was what you got, with Harry.

Harry Truman had a sign in the Oval Office that said:

> **The buck stops here!**

The country understood exactly what he was saying: I will not pass the buck. I will not scapegoat others or avoid responsibility. I will be accountable for my actions.

Harry Truman (funny, no one ever seems to refer to him as President Truman) didn't hide behind other people, or claim that a mistake of his was a political conspiracy organized by vengeful opponents to discredit him.

When he became infuriated at a snide review of his daughter's singing debut and was quoted as wanting to thrash the cad, he didn't claim afterward that he was misquoted or misunderstood or taken out of context. He cheerfully admitted that those were the sentiments of an outraged father, and he stood behind them.

WHERE DOES YOUR BUCK STOP?

There is a great trend in our country toward what has been called the Victimization Movement. Its premise is that the traumas we suffered as children render us not responsible for our actions today. This theory says that the programs we had thrust upon us in childhood are the ones by which our internal computer will run for the rest of our lives. It is embraced by a great number of mental health professionals.

In this model, Experience is Destiny.

The famous Twelve Steps of Alcoholics Anonymous show us quite another model. Those steps are about fearless honesty and accountability for behavior. Recovering AA members get quite a laugh out of remembering the days when they still said, "She drove me to it," or "It just happened." They know better now. They know that no-one forced their jaws open and poured alcohol down their throats. They are making a decision, every day of their lives, not to drink just for that day. It is a choice they make, and with the help of their Higher Power and the support of the AA group, they make it, one day at a time.

Choice and responsibility are empowering! The person who says, "They [life, circumstance] made me do it" is impotent. He sees himself as a little boat being tossed about on the wild waves of chance without oars or rudder.

Here is a whimsical parody of the twelve steps of AA, an ironic mirror version. Unfortunately, it's the unconscious creed by which many people live:

The Twelve Steps of NON-Recovery

1) We admitted we were powerless over nothing, that we would manage our lives perfectly and those of anyone else who would allow us to.

2) Came to believe that there was no power greater than ourselves and that the rest of the world was insane.

3) Made a decision to have our loved ones and friends turn their will and their lives over to our care, even though they couldn't understand us.

4) Made a searching moral and immoral inventory of everyone we knew.

5) Admitted to the whole world the exact nature of everyone else's wrongs.

6) Were entirely ready to make others straighten up and do right.

7) Demanded that others either shape up or ship out.

8) Made a list of all persons who had harmed us and became willing to go to any length to get even with them all.

9) Got direct revenge on such people whenever possible, except when to do so would cost us our lives, or at the very least, a jail sentence.

10) Continued to take the inventory of others, and when they were wrong promptly and repeatedly told them about it.

11) Sought through complaining and nagging to improve our relations with others as we couldn't understand them, asking only that they knuckle under and do it our way.

12) Having had a complete physical, emotional and spiritual breakdown as a result of these steps, we tried to blame it on others and to get sympathy and pity in all of our affairs.

We laughed out loud when we read the "steps" because we recognized how easy it is to fall into them. They are the epitome of non-responsibility for self and excessive responsibility and/or control of others. Their entire premise is built upon, "I'm OK and you're not—but not to worry, *I'll fix you."*

The truth is, the only person I have a prayer of fixing is myself.

As psychotherapists we agree that each person's model of the world was born in childhood, that little children are helpless to prevent or materially influence the world around them. However, we passionately believe that now, as a thinking, self-determining adult <u>you can choose</u> what kind of person you are going to be today and tomorrow.

You are a sentient being of sound mind and (mostly) body, and you are recreating yourself each day. You can choose to spiff up yesterday's model to be even better today.

The good news is, you are responsible for your own life. The bad news is, you are responsible for your own life. The buck stops here!

We're not saying you attracted that jalopy without brakes, being driven by a drunk without insurance, to broadside you. Not at all. You cannot control much of what life hands you.

What you *can* do is decide what you're going to do with it, without self-condemnation or scapegoating of others.

As Zukav said,

> **An authentically empowered person is incapable of making anyone or anything a victim.**

Authentic power is the inherent life force in all of us that, when recognized and validated, can energize and inspire. All our great teachers have been beings of authentic power. Christ, Buddha, Gandhi, all have spoken and acted from a sense of deepest truths, not the world's definition of status and power.

You can choose your authentic power. You can validate, encourage, and support yorself, acting from your own internal base of integrity. You can gladly accept the fact that you are the final Editor of your life, the only one with the right to edit and rewrite it till you make it come out the best you know how. The one who can choose your own passion as part of your birthright.

And the only one with the power.

PATH #3

EXPANDING YOUR COMFORT ZONE

Life is either a daring adventure or nothing.
Security does not exist in nature...
Avoiding danger is no safer
in the long run than exposure.

— Helen Keller

COEUR-AGE

To have more passion in your life, you must gather the courage to go beyond your comfort zone—that area of habitual attitudes and behaviors in which you feel secure.

"Courage" literally means "have heart." It is not the absence of fear. If there were no fear, then courage—valor in the face of trepidation—would not be necessary.

HELEN'S STORY

No greater story of courage exists than that of Helen Keller.

Born a normal child, she had a massive fever at age nine months that left her blind and deaf. Imagine that for just a moment. Imagine growing from infancy into childhood, trying to understand the world and yourself in it, without being able to hear or see. Learning through the sense of touch was all Helen could do, and it was insufficient.

When her teacher Annie Sullivan came into Helen's life, the child was like a wild animal, given to screaming, furniture-smashing tantrums of frustration. Her loving, grieving parents had handicapped her—even more than the devastation of her disabilities—by giving her no discipline of any kind. They simply expected nothing of her. There was nothing to stretch or challenge Helen except the awful burden of being alive but isolated.

Annie Sullivan had grown up in a poor-house, was herself half-blind, and was possessed of an iron determination to overcome handicaps. She became obsessed with a passion to break a doorway into the intellectual darkness in which Helen Keller lived.

NORMALIZING LIMITS

The first thing Annie did was to establish boundaries. It was no longer acceptable for Helen to range around the dinner table, scrounging food off other people's plates. She met with furious resistance from Helen, a passionate child who was fiercely determined to continue the behaviors she was used to.

They represented the only comfort zone she knew in a bewildering world.

Slowly Annie prevailed, bringing some degree of order to the chaos that had been the Keller household.

LANGUAGE IN THE PALM OF HER HAND

Helen was an extraordinarily bright child, and as she was able to become focused, she became enthralled in the alphabet game.

At least, to her it was a kind of game. Annie spelled out the letters of the alphabet into her hand, and Helen learned to imitate the signs in order to get something she wanted. The pressures in her hand were a code: If she wanted an apple, she had learned that the symbols **a-p-p-l-e** would get her an apple.

The Kellers were thrilled. It was more than they had ever expected. Helen could actually communicate her wants in a civilized way!

Now that their little wild animal was domesticated, they wanted Annie Sullivan to leave. Her stern, demanding expectations of Helen were beyond their comfort zone.

But Annie was far from satisfied. She knew that Helen still did not understand that the words in her hand weren't just a code for demanding things—they were symbols that <u>stood for</u> the things. If Helen could only learn that, then she would have language, and from language could spring learning, not only about the world around her, but about the world of ideas.

Eventually Helen reached that breakthrough. Through Annie Sullivan's passionate refusal to diminish Helen as her parents did, she brought the child out of cognitive darkness and into the light.

The passionate fury that had fueled Helen Keller's early rebellion was tranformed into the passion for knowledge and sharing with others that characterized her whole life. With Annie's help, Helen studied history, languages, literature, philosophy. In her world of the mind, she went hundreds of years and thousands of miles beyond the Keller plantation.

PUSHING THE ENVELOPE OF SAFETY

Until that point, Helen's world had remained the safe, protected world of her plantation. With enormous courage, she left that comfort zone of the familiar and went out into the world.

Helen Keller graduated with highest honors from university and went on to become a reknowned speaker and author, traveling literally all over the world with the devoted Annie Sullivan by her side. Her speech was hard to understand, since she had never heard human speech, but people came by the thousands to hear her whenever she made a public appearance. An entire generation revered her heroism as they watched her live those words:

Life is either a daring adventure or nothing. Security does not exist in nature. ...Avoiding danger is no safer in the long run than exposure.

NO FAILED EXPERIMENTS

Many years ago an educator named John Holt tried an experiment with a class of fouth-graders. He said, "Class, I am thinking of a number between one and a thousand. I want you to figure out what it is by asking me questions that can only be answered Yes or No."

The class buzzed as they conferred about the first question to ask. The kid they chose to speak for them said, "Is your number between one and five hundred?"

Great question! In one clever stroke it narrowed the field by half, regardless of his answer.

"No," answered Holt.

The whole class groaned loudly, even though they had elicited exactly the same information as if he'd said yes!

In his landmark book <u>Why Children Fail</u> Holt points out the fallacy of requiring that children anticipate what the teacher wants to hear and then give that answer, instead of approaching a problem in the true sense of inquiry.

The same principle applies to you. When you try something new, whatever the outcome, you learn from the experience. Perhaps you learn never again to believe you can change someone just by the sheer weight of your love. Or maybe you just learn a homely little lesson like, Never again will I lift something heavy out of the trunk of the car by bending forward from the waist with my knees locked.

<u>There is no such thing as failure, only feedback.</u> You aren't a stupid person for not knowing something, you're just better informed after you learn it.

THE RISK/REWARD RATIO

There *is* such a thing as an unacceptable risk, where the potential payoff is simply not worth the speculation. Your decisions in all areas of your life are influenced by your perception of the risk/reward ratio.

There is an exceedingly small chance that you'll win the lottery, but on the other hand, a dollar isn't much to risk. Would you still buy the ticket if you had a 50/50 chance of winning ten million dollars, but losing would cause you to forfeit all your belongings?

SORTING OUT YOUR VOICES

With risk/reward assessments, as with all things, you are the world's greatest living expert about you. You are the one person with the right to decide what is worth the risk of pushing beyond the comfort zone, and what is not.

The trick is to learn which of your inner Look-Out voices to trust. One voice is sending you important, reality-based information: "Driving eighty miles an hour in the rain just isn't worth the fifteen minutes you'll shave off your travel time." Even if it means you run the risk of being late to meet a plane, the risk really isn't worth the pay-off. The pay-off is being on time, the risk is possible death.

But there is that other voice—the one that tries to keep you safe by hiding out. It is the voice of fear that keeps you from getting what you really want, something that *is* worth the risk. You learned it at a very early age, and you may want to update it if it is preventing you from your healthy passion.

FEAR, THE PASSION ASSASSIN

Fear is one of the most potent emotions humans can experience. At best it's intimidating, at worst paralyzing.

It can also be transcended.

In his epic fantasy novel <u>Dune</u> Frank Herbert tells of highly disciplined people who have learned how to rise above their fear. When they feel fear descending upon them, they repeat the following mantra:

I must not fear. Fear is the mind-killer. Fear is the little-death that brings total obliteration.

I will face my fear. I will permit it to pass over and through me.

And when it has gone past, I will turn the inner eye to see its path. Where the fear has gone there will be nothing. Only I will remain.

When you face down your fear by taking small steps beyond your comfort zone, the result is an expansion of that zone. Each time you stretch yourself, you stretch the arena in which you feel confident to move.

WHAT'S YOUR WORST FEAR?

At the end of a comfortable dinner party the guests, all old friends, were drinking coffee and talking. Somebody said, "What is your greatest fear, and what would you do if it happened?"

Tina said, "I think the worst thing would be to get Lou Gehrig's disease. It's irreversible and incurable. Your motor neurons stop firing a little at a time until you end up completely paralyzed and unable even to speak. And the worst part is, your mind is as sharp as ever! You are completely present as your body is slipping away, and you can't do anything about it and neither can anyone else. If I ever got Lou Gehrig's disease, there isn't the slightest doubt in my mind that I'd commit suicide."

There was silence for a long moment. Then Jack said, "What about Stephen Hawking?"

STEPHEN HAWKING'S STORY

Professor Stephen Hawking is generally accepted to be the most brilliant theoretical physicist since Einstein. His is unquestionably one of the great minds of this or any other time. His research into black holes has greatly enhanced our understanding of the universe and provided clues to that elusive moment when the universe was born.

Stephen Hawking was still in graduate school twenty-five years ago when he was diagnosed as having ALS. He knew perfectly well what that meant.

In his case the disease initially progressed at a heartbreakingly rapid pace. When he could no longer stand, he would pull himself up the stairs by his hands and elbows, refusing any kind of help.

The disease advanced inexorably, and he was in a wheelchair in a matter of months. And his mind played on.

When his brilliant book <u>A Brief History of Time</u> was published in 1988, Timothy Ferris, the reviewer for <u>Vanity Fair</u>, said of it, "He is leaping beyond relativity, beyond quantum mechanics, beyond the big bang, to the 'dance of geometry' that created the universe."

In the book Hawking makes brief and casual reference to his disease:

Apart from being unlucky enough to get ALS, or motor neuron disease, I have been fortunate in almost every other respect.

That's how he looks at it—that ALS was bad luck and is an awkward nuisance, but it's a fact, so let's get on with life.

About ten years ago, on a PBS special on astrophysics, a segment was devoted to Hawking with a videotape of one of his lectures. Here was this wizened raisin of a man, limbs all twisted, topped by a large head and Coke-bottle glasses. When a question was asked about an equation, Hawking answered in a series of squeaks and grunts that didn't even sound like human speach, much less English. His assistant, accustomed to the sounds, translated what the professor had said. The students were all used to it, even debated some points with him. TV viewers who weren't prepared for this drama were flabbergasted—at Hawking's brilliance and courage, and at everyone's matter-of-fact acceptance of his condition.

In <u>A Brief History</u> Hawking writes:

I have had a lot of help with this book from Brian Whitt, one of my students. I caught pneumonia in 1985, after I had written the first draft. I had to have a tracheostomy operation which removed my ability to speak and made it almost impossible for me to communicate. I thought I would be unable to finish the book. However, Brian not only helped me revise it, he also got me using a communications program called Living Center. ...With this I can both write books and papers, and speak to people using a speech synthesizer.

...The synthesizer and a small personal computer were mounted on my wheelchair by David Mason. This system has made all the difference: In fact, I can communicate better now that before I lost my voice.

Time magazine said, "Even as he sits helpless in his wheelchair, his mind seems to soar ever more brilliantly across the vastness of space and time to unlock the secrets of the universe."

Marci's story is about literally stepping out of one's comfort zone and into thin air.

ONE GIANT STEP FOR MARCI

Marci and Arnold grew up in a textbook middle-class home, admonished daily by their loving mother to be careful, look before they leap, and not take silly chances.

In some ways each became a risk-taker anyway. They chose artistic, non-mainstream careers, and they trust their own inner wisdom about what is good for them.

Physically, however, they remained true to Mom's teaching. Until just a few years ago.

Path #3: Expanding Your Comfort Zone

Marci decided to start facing down her fears. First she rode on a midway ride that terrified her. Afterward she bounded off like a gazelle and didn't stop talking for days about how liberating an experience it had been.

The day she tried parasailing, a sudden wind shift dumped her into the ocean from a great height. She had some impressive bruises that lasted for weeks, and she was clearly proud of them.

The ultimate challenge was sky-diving. She first tried it a few years ago and made it through the pre-jump training and onto the jump plane, but after three passes over the jump area, she just couldn't bring herself to do it.

Then she went to visit Arnold in California and learned about a field that offered buddy-jumping. The novice is strapped spoon-fashion to an experienced instructor who does all the work, but the novice must give the okay to jump when the time comes. Marci and Arnold decided to go for it.

The videotape of that event is a study in expanding your comfort zone. Marci and Arnold are laughing and joking as they get on the plane and throughout the flight, until about ten minutes till jump time. Then they both get very quiet and their faces take on a mask-like quality.

Marci and her instructor buddy were to be first out of the plane. She says they stood in the jump door for what seemed like five minutes, waiting for her to okay the jump. Her instructor kept saying reassuring things in her ear, including the fact that she was the one who would make the decision. Right. That's what she was doing. Making the decision. Right. Still making the decision. Still making it.

Then she thought about the words of the burly, tattooed biker from the group who had jumped just before hers. He had turned to her, grinned, and said,

"Remember. Fear is optional."

That did it—that and the realization that if she chickened out now, the whole planeload might. So she said Okay to her jump partner, and out they went.

Now she says that if someone offered her a thousand dollars to erase the event, she would turn it down.

OTHER LEAPS OF FAITH

The college-aged brother and sister who decided to take their tuition money and turn a bankrupt yogurt shop around. They were 18 and 19 when they began. Three years later they were millionaires.

The 55-year-old graduate student. He says it doesn't matter how long it takes to get his degrees, he's in it more for the learning than for the letters after his name.

The young woman with heart trouble who consciously chooses to have a baby against her doctor's advice.

The 6-year-old learning to ride a bike.

And the thousands of small acts of faith, courage, and passion you have done in your own life and all the ones you will still do.

TO SUM UP ...

Why stretch beyond your comfort level if you don't have to?

Three good reasons spring to mind.

One is because you want to face down your fears for the sheer delight of defeating them. In other words, for the principle of the thing.

The second is because you want to broaden your comfort zone, have more room in which to move with ease, more freedom of choice.

The third is because you have something to gain that is important to you, something you care about passionately.

And, of course, once you have pushed out the boundaries of your comfort zone over and over, there comes a time when not very much daunts you.

> *Courage is the price that life exacts*
> *for granting peace.*
> — **Amelia Earhart**

PATH #4:

FOLLOWING YOUR BLISS

I think that what we're [all] seeking is an experience of being alive, so that our life experiences on the purely physical plane will have resonances within our most innermost being and reality, so that we actually feel the rapture of being alive.

— Joseph Campbell
<u>The Power of Myth</u>

LOVING WHAT YOU DO, DOING WHAT YOU LOVE

The luckiest people we know are the ones who are doing what they love. Maybe it's what they dedicate themselves to on weekends, getting the To-Do List out of the way as speedily as possible so they can hit the golf course, or the Boys' Club, or the easel.

Or maybe it's how they earn their daily bread, doing something for money that they like so much they'd do it for free.

THE SPACE DOCTOR

Dr. Jim Logan was head of NASA's medical operations. He was able to take two childhood passions and make both the dreams come true.

As a kid Jim was fascinated with flight. His earliest memories were of his dad taking him out to the old Tulsa airport to watch planes take off. He watched riveted as the first satellite, Sputnik, was shot into space by the Russians. He was enthralled to hear the narrator say this hunk of metal was going all the way around the earth every ninety minutes!

When he was ten, an event occurred which reshaped Jim's life forever.

> *...I read in the newspaper that a visiting astronomer was going to teach a night school class at the University of Tulsa. I casually mentioned to my parents how neat it would be to hear those lectures. My mom arranged it so I could attend those classes.*
>
> *On Monday nights from 7:00 till 9:45 I would go to this astronomy class. I was the only person under the age of 25 there; most of them were graduate students.*
>
> *Originally I was going to just observe, but when it came time to take the mid-term and the final, I felt reasonably confident that I grasped the general idea of what was going on, so I asked the professor if I could take the test. And he said (it kind of took him aback), "Well, all right."*

Jim took the test and ended up with a passing grade—not an A or B, but a passing grade in a college astronomy course. His confidence level soared.

The newspaper found out about it and did a story on me, the ten-year-old kid that took a college course in astronomy.

The manned space program was just starting. I'm sure it was part of a publicity stunt—I don't really know how this happened—but the University of Tulsa selected me to help represent them at this conference [on the peaceful use of space].

I can remember going to these exhibits with my conference kit and my little badge that said "Jim Logan" on it. Carnegie was my elementary school and so it said "Carnegie" on it. Other badges were saying Rockwell Int'l, McDonnell Douglas, University of Tulsa, and here was "Carnegie," my elementary school.

In that all-important tenth year of his life, Jim's family had a playroom built over the garage. The walls were slanted and wouldn't accommodate pictures. His mother hired a university art student to paint a mural, a project in which he got deeply involved.

I wanted her to paint a SPACESCAPE instead of a landscape. I found two books, showed her what I wanted, and she transferred some of those pictures to the wall. She'd do it in chalk first and I would make corrections because some of the stuff she did wasn't technically correct. I wanted it done right.

It was a mural of the construction of a space station. It's still there at the house. She signed her name and dated it 1961, the year I turned 11. Every time I'd go up to the playroom I would be surrounded by outer space.

Originally Jim Logan wanted to be an astronomer. A little later he found out what a physicist was and thought that's what he wanted to be. There was just one problem—the math. He was young for his grade level and in an accelerated math class, and he was scared.

I didn't do very well and it really shattered my self-confidence. It was the first time in my life I had ever come to terms with the fact that I just might be stupid in an area. It really shook me up.

He rediscovered his confidence when he got turned on to chemistry and then biology. It was a natural progression. He had always liked the out-of-doors, and the idea of working with organic, living systems began to take precedence over the idea of space.

When we landed a man on the moon in 1969, Jim was about to start his sophomore year. About then, he decided to be a doctor. The NASA space coverage included talk about Dr. Charles Barry, physician to the astronauts. And Jim thought, "That's it! That's what I want to do."

Path #4: Following Your Bliss

The space program went to college with Jim. Instead of pin-ups on his bulletin board, he had photos of the astronauts on the moon.

I had a record of a Mission Control launch scenario, and I used to listen to it for hours and visualize what it would be like to work in Mission Control. I'd play a scene over and over again and feel the tension before the rocket went up. Is it going to work? Is it going to function right? I'd focus my attention, not just listen to the record but very intently see it and feel it.

By 1974 the space program seemed all but ended, but it stayed in the back of Jim's mind as he graduated from medical school.

In October of 1978, during his surgery internship, Jim took his first look at OMNI magazine. It seemed tailor-made for him. He took his beeper, went up to the hospital roof, and read OMNI cover to cover. This is how he remembers it:

I decided right then that life was just too short and that I needed more. I said to myself, I don't know what I'm going to be doing this time next year, but I won't be here. I'll finish my internship and then I'm leaving. I've got do something that excites me.

This gave me a tremendous release, put me back in touch with the child part that had had those fantasies. All of a sudden I just felt infused with energy. My powers of concentration were crystal clear. I kept visualizing what kind of environment I wanted to be in, and I knew I wanted to work in the space program."

Jim hit a few snags but ultimately was accepted into a new aerospace medicine residency program. He spent two years in the Dayton program and the third year at the Johnson Space Center in Houston. He had this strange sense of *deja' vu*. He had done it all before! In his childhood, by visualizing it.

Jim Logan's passion took him from that garage-room mural to NASA, designing the medical facility on board the space station. He was able to merge his love of the space program, medicine, technology, computers, and aviation all into one thrilling vocation.

THE GREEK CONNECTION

In an affluent suburb there lived a professional couple in their mid-30s; he was a litigation lawyer, she a highly-paid management consultant. They had a huge house and drove very expensive sports cars. Although they made six figures each, the cost of their standard of living ate up every cent they made.

One day they stopped and realized that their life wasn't satisfying them. There was very little real pleasure in their lives and no time to cherish the relationship they had once delighted in. They sat down with legal pads and pens and asked themselves what, at the age of 85, they would regret not having done.

Path #4: Following Your Bliss

Each came up with the same conclusion: what they both longed to do was live in a foreign culture and have more time just for life.

They had no major obligations other than the financial tiger they had by the tail. The set about reducing their belongings to what was absolutely essential or very dear to them, and they moved to a Greek island, where they rented a little one-bedroom house.

Instead of luxury cars, they now drive a third-hand Russian jeep. Shopping for dinner ingredients begins at the wharf, buying fish from the the fisherman who caught it. Bread comes still warm from the baker's oven, and the vegetables they buy were still growing last night. The only grocery store on the island is the size of a corner convenience store back in the States.

She now works as a painter and printmaker. He writes columns and articles about their life and gives seminars all over Europe and the United States about following the deep desires of one's heart.

"It isn't about moving to a new culture," they say. "That just happens to have been our own dream. It's about honoring your dream and making it a reality."

Their workshops are very successful. So are they, though not in the way the folks back in the half-million-dollar houses might judge.

They have never been so happy in their lives. To them, sharing bread and cheese with friends around a wood fire on the beach at sunset—that's wealth.

PASSION! Reclaiming the Fire in Your Heart

GUERRILLA GOODNESS

Following your bliss doesn't have to take you down a new career path or move you to a foreign culture. Anne Herbert, a writer who lives in Berkeley, California, enriched her own culture when she created this slogan:

> Practice random kindness
> and senseless acts of beauty.

Ordinary people of all kinds have felt those words resonate within them and are moving gently through their little corners of the world, doing such small anonymous kindnesses as putting coins in expired parking meters.

Although Ms. Herbert wrote the phrase in 1982, is has only been in the last couple of years that it has caught fire. The story was carried anonymously on a computer bulletin board and writted up in <u>Reader's Digest</u>.

Here is an excerpt from that E-mail version:

> *It's a crisp winter day in San Francisco. A woman in a red Honda, Christmas presents piled in the back, drives up to the Bay Bridge tollbooth. "I'm paying for myself and for the six cars behind me," she says with a smile, handling over seven commuter tickets. One after*

another, the next six drivers arrive at the tollbooth, dollars in hand, only to be told, "Some lady up ahead already paid your fare. Have a nice day."

The woman in the Honda, it turned out, had read on an index card taped to a friend's refrigerator the phrase, "Practice random kindness and senseless acts of beauty."

Judy Foreman spotted the same phrase spray-painted on a warehouse wall a hundred miles from her home. ..."I thought it was incredibly beautiful," she said, explaining why she's taken to writing it at the bottom of all her letters, "like a message from above."

Her husband Frank liked the phrase so much that he put it up on the wall for his seventh-graders. One was the daughter of a local columnist who put it in the paper, admitting that though she liked it, she didn't know where it came from or what it really meant. Two days later she heard from [its author] Anne Herbert [who] had jotted the phrase down on a paper placemat. "That's wonderful!" a man sitting nearby said, and copied it down carefully on his own placemat.

It is positive anarchy, disorder, a sweet disturbance. A woman in Boston writes "Merry Christmas" to the tellers on the backs of her checks. A man in St. Louis, whose car has just been rear-ended by a young woman, waves her away, saying, "It's just a scratch. Don't worry."

Senseless acts of beauty spread. A man plants daffodils along the roadway, his shirt billowing in the breeze from passing cars. In Seattle a man appoints *himself a one-man sanitation service and roams the concrete hills collecting litter in a supermarket cart. In Atlanta a man scrubs graffitti from a green park bench.*

...If you were one of those rush-hour drivers who found your bridge fare paid, who knows what you might have been inspired to do for someone else later. Wave someone on in the intersection? Smile at a tired clerk? Or something larger, greater?

Like all revolutions, guerrilla goodness begins slowly, with a single act.

LIFE AS AN ART FORM

Decide, just for today, to do something that delights you, even if it doesn't ring your chimes till your bones vibrate. Maybe it will be a random kindness, a senseless act of beauty. Or perhaps a short visit to a long-neglected past passion.

A woman once said wistfully to her painter friend, "I wish I were an artist." He answered, "But my dear, you are—and life is your medium."

Perhaps that is the ultimate bliss—loving the act of living and bringing creativity and vitality to it.

I'd rather teach one bird to sing
than teach 10,000 stars how not to dance.
— e. e. cummings

PATH #5

AFFIRMING THE <u>YES!</u> TO LIFE

"[Passion for life is] a universal hunger that pervades the world. It is the hunger to get more out of life, to give more back, to be more involved and to find more meaning. This is the hunger of the soul searching for something more."

— Muriel James
<u>Passion for Life</u>

Nadine Stair of Louisville, Kentucky, wrote in her 85th year about the importance of play. Her words have become familiar to millions of people as a recipe for living life with presence and passion.

If I had my life to live over I'd dare to make more mistakes the next time. I'd relax. I would limber up. I would be sillier than I have been on this trip. I would take more chances. I would take more trips. I would climb more mountains and swim more rivers. I would eat more ice cream and less beans. I would perhaps have more actual troubles, but I would have fewer imaginary ones.

You see, I am one of those people who live sensibly and sanely, hour after hour, day by day. Oh, I've had my moments, and if I had it to do over again, I'd have more of them. In fact, I'd try to have nothing else—just moments, one after another, instead of living so many years ahead of each day. I have been one of those persons who never goes anywhere without a thermometer, a hot water bottle, a raincoat and a parachute. If I had it to do again, I'd travel lighter than I have.

If I had my life to live over, I would start barefoot earlier in the spring and stay that way later in the fall. I'd wade in more mud puddles. I would go to more dances. I would ride more merry-go-rounds. I would pick more daisies.

Suppose death brought enlightenment and you could go back as a guardian guide to the younger You, the You who is still living. Imagine what wisdom you'd want to share.

Path #5: Affirming the YES! to Life

It might sound a lot like Nadine's. It's hard to think of an enlightened guide suggesting that you spend more time obsessing about your "security" and less living each moment.

Wouldn't you advise yourself to take life more seriously and yourself less seriously?

Let's examine some of Nadine's suggestions.

> I'd relax.

Parents of several children usually say they were uptight with the first, then increasingly relaxed with each subsequent child. Of course, the first kid feels too controlled (and probably is) and the last can feel neglected (though often becomes wise enough to see that less parenting is generally better). The relaxed (experienced) parent knows that grass stains on the knees of chinos are no big deal, that a mistake is a learning opportunity, and that somehow, literally and figuratively, it'll mostly all come out in the wash.

One mother said, "With my first child, if she dropped her bottle on the floor, I would replace the nipple with a sterilized one. With my third, I just picked the dog hair off it and handed it back to the kid in the high chair."

Such an attitude sends a message that backyard picnics are more important than polishing silver, and that leaving three books around because you're reading all three is better than always having every book neatly shelved and unread.

> I'd be sillier.

There was a woman who gave a Twelfth-Night party one January 5, and for the invitation she rewrote <u>The Twelve Days of Christmas</u> song to read:

**On the Twelfth Day of Christmas
my true love sent to me:**

**12 strippers glitzing
11 seltzers spritzing
10 shrinks a-shrinking
9 bubbas drinking**

... well, you get the idea. She challenged the guests to come dressed as one of the twelve days.

Everyone got a chance at creative silliness of the highest (lowest?) order. The results were memorable.

One woman dressed in neck-to-floor black and wore a glittery silver top hat. She was a seltzer spritzing.

There were several discreet strippers, the most innovative of whom was a medical illustrator who put on a skin-colored bodysuit which she had painstakingly painted with the entire human vascular system—intricate roadways of red and blue veins and arteries—so that she seemed to be walking around without skin. Now that's <u>stripping</u>.

One man put on a gimme cap, tied empty beer cans around his neck, and came as a bubba drinking. He referred often to his pickup truck and started conversations with, "Well, darlin', like I was tellin' Jim Bob the other ev'nin'..."

The most spectacular guest was a gentleman we'll call Steve, a quiet, dignified comptroller for a major company. Steve put on a wig, gorgeous makeup, a well-endowed bosom, and a stunning dress. Although he was a little wobbly in his size eleven high heels, he almost gave Dolly Parton a run for her money.

Silly? Of course! Like all costume parties, the guests got to be playful kids with a just a touch of mischief, and any lingering post-Christmas let-down got cleared right away.

By the way, the only Day of Christmas not represented was 10 shrinks a-shrinking, although half a dozen guests were counselors. They preferred to be somebody else for an evening.

> **I would ride more merry-go-rounds.**

If you want to find a mentor to help you recapture your sense of wonder, to savor and fully live in the moment, look no farther than a child.

Pat says, "When my passion for life is temporarily pooped, I borrow my best friends' children. Richard and Jane are my barometers on life's joy and possibilities. The delight they have in this world is infectious, so when I'm running low, I go absorb some of their energy and wonder."

She particularly savors the memory of the afternoon she took them to see the animated film Beauty and the Beast. At the end of it she asked Richard what he learned from the movie. He looked up at her with luminous brown eyes and said, "I learned that you can never be ugly if you have love in your heart."

It was a passing moment for small Richard, but to his grown-up friend Pat it is a memory she still cherishes and a truth to appreciate.

> I would have moments, one after another...

At home on a spring evening just before sunset, Roz got a phone call from Robert, who said, "Go out and look high up in the northern sky." She went out into the back yard, and there, hanging motionless against the sky, was an iridescent celestial pearl.

It shimmered like mercury and was as creamy as a full moon, though only an eighth the size. It really did look like a mysterious, impossibly luminous pearl.

She ran back to the phone and gasped, "What is it?!" and he answered, "Sweetheart, it's a weather balloon, miles up." She thanked him for it and then said, "I've got to hang up now and go back and watch it."

Path #5: Affirming the YES! to Life

She dragged out an old aluminum lawn chaise, got a pillow to support her neck, and lay back to watch the pearl.

The sun went down and still the pearl shimmered against the darkening sky. Only when the sky turned to deep blue-purple did the pearl begin to change color, as it finally started to reflect the setting sun that had descended below the horizon almost an hour earlier.

The pearl took on a whisper of pink, then a decided shell-pink, then a watermelon hue, then a deeper coral, then brilliant orange, then red, deeper red, a dark blood-red, and finally it disappeared against the black sky.

The entire magical performance had taken two hours.

To this day Roz carries that cosmic pearl in her consciousness. She imagines it dwells within her, gently pulsing somewhere behind her navel, glowing in the dark.

> ...instead of living so many years ahead of each day.

In his brilliantly eccentric book, <u>Mine Enemy Grows Older</u>, artist/writer Alexander King says:

> *Only two weeks ago, the son of a friend of mine was offered a fine job by the General Electric Company. He still hasn't made up his mind, because he wants to make sure that they guarantee him the most satisfactory*

retirement fund available in today's labor market. He's going to be twenty-two years old next December.

I have nothing to say in disparagement of such an attitude; it just doesn't interest me. It never did. ...The great joys and the true ecstasies in my life came from surprises and achievements which were the results of certain risks that I was willing to take.

Alex King himself, a Hungarian immigrant, lived his whole life as an adventure. He seemed to attract strange characters and surreal situations, all of which he hugely enjoyed. His book is filled with the lively tales of a supreme livelover for whom old age security was a *very* low priority.

> **I would take more chances.**

Perhaps the adults in your childhood sent you lots of LOOK OUT! messages, told you to be very careful and not to hope for too much so you wouldn't be too disappointed. Of course they meant well, but look how those messages may have inhibited you.

There is another way to raise kids. A mother once said, "Don't worry about my son climbing the tree. It's true, he could fall and break an arm, but he's actually very good at shinnying

Path #5: Affirming the YES! to Life

up that old tree—and besides, I like it that he'd rather risk breaking an arm than be scared to climb."

That adventuresome little Tom Sawyer is grown now and still climbing, still seeking adventures, still calling his own shots and trusting in himself.

Consider the thought of giving <u>yourself</u> encouraging, go-for-it! messages today.

> **I would perhaps have more actual troubles,
> but I would have fewer imaginary ones.**

All fear is futurizing. Most of the scary stories we tell ourselves never come true anyway—but even if some of them do, why let the imagined future contaminate the lovely present?

When you're apprehensive about a possible risk, ask yourself, What's the worst-case scenario? Can I live with that? And what's the <u>best</u> that might happen—how would I handle *that?*

WAKE UP!

Even if you aren't accustomed to doing it, you can learn to be really aware, alive, awake to the process of Life.

There is a story about the Buddha that goes like this:

A student met the Buddha on the road one day and asked him:
"Are you a God?"
"No, I'm not."
"Are you an angel?"
"No, I'm not."
"Then, what are you?"
"I'm awake, that's all. I'm just *awake*."

IN A NUTSHELL—

As you walk down this path to passion, you will find three messages. When you can heed them all, you have traversed the path. They are:

---

*Cherish your curiosity
and capacity for wonder.*

Savor the familiar and honor the strange.

Live your life fully and enjoy it passionately.

PATH #6

TRUSTING THE INNER CLICK

EXPECT A MIRACLE!

According to a survey conducted by the Religious Broadcasters Association, eight out of ten Americans believe in miracles.

As with most surveys, the target group's preconceived values colored the outcome. Still, virtually everyone has experienced that personal miraculous event we're calling the *Inner Click*. It is a paradigm shift, a sudden change in perception as dramatic as the optometrist's lens. "Which is better? This? or THIS."

You are trudging along in your life, walking a path so familiar that it's approaching rut-hood, when a miracle happens. The right event or person or **a-ha!** shows up, and you hear or feel that Inner Click—that lightbulb experience—of rightness, of recognition.

ENTER KAIROS

The younger generation asks the older, "How will I know?" How will I know when I am in love, when I'm ready to choose a career, when I'm ready to leave home? And the answer comes, "You'll know."

It isn't that simple, of course, because all events are part of process. Still, in addition to the familiar *chronos*—linear, clock-and-calendar time—there really is *kairos: the moment of sweet internal ripeness.*

> *There is this to remember about Passion.*
> *It lives in the kairos time zone.*

Kairos is to *chronos* as right brain is to left, as hand-crafted is to machine-made. Here's what Sam Keen says about it in his book, To a Dancing God:

The industrial revolution began symbolically with the invention of the portable clock, when the tick-tock of mechanical chronology replaced the sun and the passing seasons as the index of time. In the era of the sundial, the rhythm of desire and satisfaction, planting and harvest, energy and fatigue encouraged human action to break forth in the time of ripeness. Kairos, rather than chronos—the prepared moment rather than the correct moment—governed life.

...Who can deny that it is well for trains to run on schedule, for meetings to begin promptly, for efficiency to be measured by time studies? Each of us has but a limited time to inhabit the earth, and should it not be used profitably? By ordering time in abstract modules, we have gained the regularity necessary to live with the machines we have created. And we have been rewarded with what we unquestionably consider "a higher standard of living." But what have we lost in the transition?

Perhaps when we ceased to measure time by the sun and the seasons, it was wisdom that suffered.

There is an ancient tradition which defines wisdom as the sense of timeliness and appropriateness.

THE HUNDREDTH MONKEY

No one knows why or how enough bits of information or intuition come together to create the Click, the internal completeness, the realization of *kairos*. A few years ago there were investigators who believed that the Click was explained by the Hundredth Monkey theory.

This notion arose from a story about a tribe of monkeys living on an island. One of the mature female monkeys discovered by accident that she could wash a particular tuber that grew in the area and make it palatable to eat. She showed all the other monkeys how to do it, and eventually the whole tribe was washing the roots and eating them.

The miraculous part was, about the time the hundredth monkey (give or take a few monkeys) learned how to wash the root, suddenly monkeys on the mainland began to do the same thing, though none of them had ever seen it. Hence the Hundredth Monkey theory, which holds that when enough bits (or participants, or sets of energy) have achieved a new perception, the whole (tribe, group, society) will get it *(kairos)*.

Actually, the hundredth Monkey story turned out to be a kind of New Age fable, never scientifically validated. However, the wisdom of ages has been passed down in the form of metaphors, parables, fables, legends, for time out of mind. A story can create a paradigm shift in the listener, a CLICK in the perception, and *voila!* a new way of thinking emerges.

One concept that emerged from the Hundredth Monkey theory was a parallel belief that if enough people on earth were to visualize and work toward world peace, a kind of critical mass of awareness could be reached by which the collective human consciousness would evolve to a higher, less primitive and aggressive state. It is a hopeful thought. Mankind's consciousness has evolved in many ways and perhaps someday will outgrow dangerous hostility. In its own way the idea is incontrovertibly true right now—one person at a time, people do create changes in their own small spheres of influence.

By the way, as a postscript to the Hundredth Monkey story, it's fascinating to note in scientific journals many incidents of what has been called the cluster effect of scientific breakthroughs. Scientists work along linear time, often without knowledge of other people's work, and suddenly they achieve simultaneous results. Nobel prizes for science have been co-awarded to teams working independently of each other who made the same discovery, almost at the same moment.

In attempts not to look superstitious, researchers have devised some extremely inventive explanations for such events. There was, for example, the puzzling phenomenon that after unsuccessful attempts in many labs to get a particular substance to crystalize, it finally did—and in a very short <u>chronological</u> time it was crystalizing in labs around the world.

The entertaining explanation put forth by some researchers was that lab workers were transporting microscopic crystals embedded in their lab coats—even though there were very few documented cases of workers visiting back and forth between labs.

WHEN THE PENNY DROPS

There was a boy who graduated from high school without knowing what he wanted to "do" with his life. He moved into an apartment with some other guys, got a series of subsistence jobs, grew up a bit. He enrolled in junior college a couple of times, then dropped the courses. He was still seeking his direction.

He moved to Vermont and learned the carpenter's trade and liked it, but he always knew it was a waystation. Then one day it came to him, like the penny dropping in an old-time gumball machine, that he wanted to be a doctor. There was absolutely no doubt in his mind.

He took out student loans, enrolled in the University of Vermont, and spent the next four years taking pre-med courses while working as a resident advisor in the dorm, doing lab research, and picking up whatever other jobs he could. He even made time to be active in the student senate, and still was able to study for his M-Cat, the pre-med exam.

He was accepted to several good medical schools, chose the one that best fitted him, and is now in his third year of medical school. All on student loans, grants in aid, and hard work.

He has never deviated. His own inner Click was like a compass that pointed unwaveringly to a point on the dial marked **Doctor**.

The painter Georgia O'Keeffe changed her life after teaching in Canyon, Texas, and visiting New Mexico. There was something about those plains and skies that *clicked* in her heart. She was so moved by the experience that she moved from New York City, where all her previous connections were, and settled in the New Mexico desert to live with a landscape unlike any she had ever known.

She wrote to a good friend:

Tonight I walked into the sunset. The whole sky— and there is so much of it out here—was just blazing, and grey blue clouds were riding all through the holiness of it. ...But some way or other I didn't seem to like the redness much, [so when] I walked home I kept walking. ...The Eastern sky was all grey blue. Bunches of clouds, different kinds of clouds, sticking around everywhere and the whole thing lit up, first in one place, then in another, with flashes of lightning—sometimes just sheet lightning, and sometimes sheet lightning with a sharp bright zigzag flashing across it.

...You see there was nothing but sky and flat prairie land, land that seems more like the ocean than anything else I know.

...I am loving the plains more than ever, it seems. And the SKY—Anita, you have never seen SKY—it is wonderful.

Georgia O'Keeffe loved that lonely spaciousness, those sparse shapes, the browns, pinks and oranges of earth and air, for more than fifty years, till the day she died.

KAIROS IN THE CORPORATE WORLD

There are corporate leaders who know all about *kairos* even if that isn't what they call their own personal Click.

In his book Never Fight With a Pig Peter Thomas tells about the moment he heard from a friend about the concept of franchised real estate brokerages.

He said that his friend Art Bartlett was packaging advertising, hiring and training services with a national image and offering the package to small real estate brokers for a percentage of their commission.

> *...I felt a rush of adrenaline go through me as I grasped the concept...It combined two old ideas: real estate and franchising. Soon I was brushing off the sand, placing a phone call to Art Bartlett and leaving the conference for Los Angeles on the first plane I could catch that day.*

Peter Thomas never doubted the rightness of his Inner Click. He ended up with ownership of Century 21 Real Estate Canada, a business he passionately enjoys. He doesn't discount the part luck played, but he says forcefully, "It was not luck that put me on that plane to California to clinch the deal for the Canadian territory; that's called seizing the opportunity. The lucky part was that the timing was perfect."

CULTIVATING THE CLICK

Sometimes the Click doesn't seem to want to come, and we get very frustrated listening for it. "Ssshh, just a minute—did you hear something?" You can put your life on Hold indefinitely at those times.

If the Click won't come unbidden, and it won't come bidden either, it's time for strategy.

When the inside-out approach (Click first, then action) has gotten stuck, you have another alternative. Take the outside-in approach.

As the Nike commercial says, *JUST DO IT !*

Without waiting for your muse to speak or inspiration to strike, just do it. Pick a place and start. Pay attention to what happens, not only in the outcome, but in your feeling about the process.

Be like the fireman who remembered one day that he he'd loved art as a kid but had lost it somewhere along the way. Just as an experiment he bought some oils and brushes and a few boards to practice on, and started slinging paint around. Now he spends hours a day in the studio he created from his garage. Where there used to be a garage door there now are north-facing French doors that flood his easels with light. He knows he isn't a terribly good painter yet, but it doesn't matter. He loves to paint.

Maybe one of your small experimental acts will be the last little bit you needed to jump-start your own Inner Click. Even if that doesn't happen, you'll have been *at choice* in your life, fine-tuning the rhythm of your own music.

Tomorrow you may dance!

PATH #7

UNITING YOUR HEAD AND HEART

Inside all of us there is a place
of perfect balance, of peace and harmony.
If you feel a twinge of skepticism,
think about it a minute.
You already know about this.

— Roz Van Meter
<u>Life Savor</u>

REALITY—WHAT A CONCEPT!

People have known for thousands of years that what you think creates your perception of life. An event itself does not have the power to create our attitude. If it did, the same event would evoke identical feelings in everyone.

It is the experience in our heads, created by our inner self-talk, that produces our uniquely personal reality.

Attitude is based on our interpretation of life events. Fortunes have been made by teaching techniques for harnessing inner attitude and directing it in healthy, life-affirming ways.

So why do we still struggle with our negative attitudes?

The answer is that there is no one formula to free us from our own self-harassment. Such liberation is an acquired skill that takes years of trial and error, negotiating around life's challenges and monitoring our interpretations of these events. This is *brain work!* It requires that we tap our own intelligence and choose thoughtfully how we will talk to ourselves.

A resolution of will is not enough. Neither is mastering life-affirming techniques. We must use them consistently, not just know about them. Like the athlete and musician and woodworker, we have to perfect our skills, including the ability to stay in shape mentally. If we nurture our attitudinal health, we can be prepared, instead of hopelessly out of shape, when a crisis or an opportunity arises.

RATIONAL CHOICES CAN NURTURE PASSION

Rationality seems at first glance to be the polar opposite of passion. Passion is emotion, calm rationality is dispassion. Used purposefully, however, dispassion can be the greatest protector and ally of passion.

USE YOUR HEAD!

You are the one who chooses what you will do with your life, one precious moment at a time.

Suppose you decide that you want more *joie de vivre* in your life, more fun and pleasure. You want to live your life more fully, not let it drift past nor watch it from the sidelines. Now the weekend is approaching and you have some choices to make. Chores? Fun? A combination of them both? Making chores fun? Doing chores first and then having fun? Having fun first? You're the one who gets to decide. Just stay aware that you do decide, and if you simply "let it happen," that is a decision.

TIME AND ENERGY

If the stained glass artist wants to work on his window, he may have to hang out a "Do Not Disturb" sign on his studio and miss the pizza-and-beer-fest.

Kathy is passionate about her two wonderful little boys. She takes enormous delight in listening to them, watching them, and sharing experiences with them. If she wants to spend the afternoon with them at the zoo, she may have to leave the dishes in the sink and let them postpone their homework till after dinner.

There is just so much energy. There is just so much time. Everything we do requires both.

Time and energy are the coin of our life, and we all have to choose how we will spend them.

SPENDING YOUR LIFE FORCE

Henry David Thoreau said, "The cost of a thing is the amount of what I call *life* which is required to be exchanged for it, immediately or in the long run."

That's absolutely true, isn't it? Just as we all have the same amount of time, and as much energy as we choose or are able to muster, we have just so many units of life force. There is a price of admission for everything. It behooves us to get our money's worth.

An interior designer once said, "Space is the new luxury. Before you acquire something, ask yourself if you want it more than the space it displaces." If we could be as deliberate about choosing our life/time/lifetime as we do in decorating our space, we'd get more bang for the buck (so to speak). We'd be less likely to want to exchange that moment, or event, or decade, for another.

WHO'S IN THE DRIVER'S SEAT?

When you were a child, maybe your granddad let you sit on his lap and pretend to steer the car. Maybe he was even reckless enough to let you do it while he was driving down the road, but he was really the one in control. His hands were hovering an inch beyond the wheel, ready to take over instantly.

Well, think about this. The little kid inside you sometimes wants to drive. And maybe you allow the little tyke's hands on the wheel sometimes. But what you'd better not do is let the child actually drive the car.

There are many moments when you will let your <u>emotions</u> make your decisions, and that will be the right thing

Path #7: Uniting Your Head and Heart

to do. There are other times when you'll <u>use your head</u>, purposefully choosing what is really in your own best interest.

Sometimes it will mean answering that ringing call: "Seize the moment!" Other times it will require postponing immediate gratification for the longer-term payoff.

WHICH DOG TO FEED

In her wise little book <u>Courage My Love</u> author Merle Shain tells the folktale of an Indian youth who sought counsel from the shaman of the tribe. The young brave was troubled because of the war in his head. "One part of me wants to travel east and another part wants to travel west. What shall I do?"

The old man was familiar with the problem. "Within each man," he said, "live two dogs. Both are strong and fight for the man's heart, one to go east and one to go west.

"The man chooses which dog will win by deciding which dog he will feed."

Here is Terry's reminiscence about a remarkable young woman and her choices about which dog-in-her-head to feed.

MARGARET'S STORY

I will never forget Margaret.

I was eighteen and still in college, and she was a twenty-three-old "career woman." Her job on our small-town newspaper seemed glamorous to her friends.

Glamorous job or not, it was apparent that Margaret was pretty poor. She lived in Mrs. Forrester's house in a rented room with kitchen privileges. She brown-bagged her lunch and never bought anyone else's coffee, though she always paid for her own. Very occasionally she would go with us to a movie, although for entertainment back then we usually had conversation and a little cheap wine. Mostly Margaret worked, borrowed books from the library, and cooked her dinner at Mrs. Forrester's house. Her only visible expenditure beyond absolute necessities was for a second-hand radio that had been left for repairs and never reclaimed.

Ten months later Margaret sold her ancient car, told us all good-bye, and left for Europe. She had been saving every nonessential dime so she could live in Paris for several months while she hunted for a job in Europe.

She found one, putting out a newspaper on a U.S. Army base, of which there were many at that time. She made twice what she'd earned at home, bought a little Volkwagen beetle, was able to purchase discounted food and clothes and gas through the PX, and spent every other weekend exploring the countryside of France, Germany and all their European neighbor countries.

As we friends started comparing notes, we realized that Margaret had always had a profound interest in Paris, the French language, and travel. Beneath her tailored clothes and serene demeanor, a quiet passion burned. She didn't talk about it much, but the dream was in there, and she marched resolutely toward it.

I think of Margaret every now and then, when I'm deciding whether to delay immediate gratification for a *longer-range goal. I imagine her looking at the menu at a hamburger and Coke and then saying to herself, "Nope, I'd rather wait for a croissant and cafe au lait on the Champs Elysee."*

Thanks, Margaret.

ENJOYING THE TRIP

When your inner gyroscope is balanced, you honor your heart by using your head. The space doctor took twenty years to bring a spacescape mural into the reality of a NASA position. How did he manage to do that?

Probably by enjoying the trip. The trip is as thrilling as the destination. When you're reaching for something you truly love, whether it's work or play or just the act of living, even the reaching-for is a joy.

The masters in the art of living make little distinction between their work and their play, their labor and their leisure, their minds and their bodies, their information, their recreation, their love and their religion. They hardly know which is which. They simply pursue their vision of excellence at whatever they do, leaving others to decide whether they are working or playing.

— James Michener

CHAPTER 8

PASSIONATE LOVE

*...and it's you are whatever a moon has always meant
and whatever a sun will always sing is you*

*here is the deepest secret nobody knows
(here is the root of the root and the bud of the bud
and the sky of the sky of a tree called life, which grows
higher than soul can hope or mind can hide)
and this is the wonder that's keeping the stars apart*

i carry your heart (i carry it in my heart)

— e. e. cummings

Love poems. Love songs. Love stories. If we stopped being interested in love and romance, much of our literature, theatre, art, movies, and songs would be obliterated.

So, what is this thing called love? What creates romantic passion? Can we keep it going forever?

TOO HOT NOT TO COOL DOWN

Most of us have known at least once the hot passion we call "being in love." Even though we know intellectually that the early phases of infatuation—mooniness, distractedness, the belief that no one else has ever loved this deeply—are a type of temporary insanity (usually benign but not always), we treasure the experience and its memory and we grieve when it is gone.

On beginning a new love affair, a friend said, "I love the thrill of it. The joy of anticipating every meeting and moment. The delight of encountering a new You with the new Him. That kind of passion gives my life new meaning and deliciousness. Without it, life can be one long dental appointment."

This kind of hot chemistry charges us with new energy, creates an excitement that can move us to great heights of love and tenderness—or jealousy and craziness.

PASSION *THROUGH* ANOTHER PERSON

All too often, what we've actually been in love with is the idea of love, or the idealized projection we have superimposed onto our loved one. The real beloved is the passion itself, and sometimes we delude ourselves for years just to keep that sense of passion alive. We are too inexperienced or short-sighted or needy to realize that in order to be in love and stay in love, you first have to learn how to be, whether in love or not.

Otherwise, we are (unconsciously) strapping onto the love affair, or the other person, the burden of making us happy. And that's too heavy a load to carry without something, or someone, collapsing.

PASSION *WITH* ANOTHER PERSON

If we begin by already having a love for life itself and not needing anyone else to complete us, we may have the great good fortune to convert infatuation to enduring, committed love. Or the wisdom to begin by growing, instead of falling, into love.

Of course, we first have to choose a partner who is willing to take responsibility for his or her own happiness, so we don't buy into a lifetime of resuscitating someone else.

Two people who choose to live life with vigor and joy, and who remain steadfast friends, can have a lifetime of adventure. Such people really share their relationship, each contributing to the emotional environment that enriches them.

ATTRACTION AND SELECTION

How do we even begin to choose our loving partners? What internal antenna is at work?

There are two general notions about partner selection: one is that the choice is psychological, and the other that it's biological/biochemical.

We hear that the "right chemistry" is a prerequisite to the right love, and it's at least partially true. Time magazine took a technical look at love's biochemistry in its February 15, 1993 cover story on the "Chemistry of Love."

> *Lovers often claim that they feel as if they are being swept away. They're not mistaken; they are literally flooded by chemicals, research suggests. A meeting of eyes, a touch of hands or a whiff of scent sets off a flood that starts in the brain and races along the nerves and through the blood. The results are familiar: flushed skin, sweaty palms, heavy breathing. If love looks suspiciously like stress, the reason is simple: the chemical pathways are identical.*
>
> *Above all, there is the sheer euphoria of falling in love, a not-so-surprising reaction considering that many of the substances swamping the newly smitten are chemical cousins of amphetamines, including dopamine, norepinephrine and especially PEA, phenylethylamine. Cole Porter knew what he was talking about when he wrote "I get a kick out of you."*

This biochemical reaction can be triggered by psychological experiences. In his excellent book, <u>Getting the Love You Want</u>, Harville Hendrix describes the "Imago" match, the choice of a lover based on early experiences that need to be resolved or repeated. The Imago partner is a person with whom you have a deep sense of recognition, one who has both positive and negative traits of people from your past.

Hendrix describes a happy mariage as

> *... a psychological and spiritual journey that begins in the ecstasy of attraction, meanders through the rocky stretch of self-discovery, and culminates in the creation of an intimate, joyful, lifelong union. Whether or not you realize the full potential of this vision depends not on your ability to attract the perfect mate, but on your willingness to acquire knowledge about the hidden parts of yourself.*

His books are well worth reading, especially if you tend to choose unwisely over and over. You may be making unconscious choices fueled by hidden desires and automatic behaviors left over from childhood. A conscious marriage can help you satisfy your leftover emotional needs in positive ways.

PASSION AND ROMANCE

We know some couples who devote loving energy to keeping romance in their relationship. They still create surprises for each other. They appreciate and acknowledge each other's efforts. They are in love with the other's body, not figure or physique—with personhood, not appearance. Thus, time cannot wither their perception of each other.

When these people fight, they fight equally and honorably. They do not demean each other, they just get it all said (sometimes at the top of their lungs) and then find an accommodation and kiss and make up.

They are delightful to be around because they enjoy each other, and more importantly, they enjoy themselves. As the saying goes, even when they are alone they're in good company.

They are complete people who choose and enjoy each other but do not need the other to be whole.

Perhaps you have seen very old couples walking down the street hand in hand or deeply involved in conversation during the intermission at a concert. They seem so young to be so old.

RUTH AND GARSON: THE LOVE AFFAIR OF A LIFETIME

One of our favorite love stories is that of actress Ruth Gordon and her director husband Garson Kanin. She was eighteen years older than he; when they fell in love and married, he was 29 and she was 47.

Together they created and produced Broadway plays, wrote screenplays, and enjoyed cherished friendships with some of the most fascinating characters of the century, among whom were Spencer Tracy and Katherine Hepburn.

Ruth Gordon and Garson Kanin lived and loved together until she was in her nineties, and he was holding her hand when she died.

Did you miss knowing Ruth Gordon? Then we urge you to rent a video of the film <u>Harold and Maude</u>. We suspect that the eccentric character she played, the epitome of *joie de vivre,* was a lot like herself.

THE REARRANGED MARRIAGE

Not everybody is lucky enough to have a Kanin-Gordon lifelong love affair. What about when it doesn't work out?

Some people are able to salvage and even revitalize a relationship that's heading south. One couple says, "We realized that we had used up the relationship we began with. Because we'd both changed, it was no longer relevant. We had to say goodbye to it and then either end it or <u>recreate it</u> into a new one." They chose the latter, and after fifteen years they're on their third version. Will they still be together in fifteen more? They are determined to be, but who knows?

THE PRICE OF PASSION

And what of the love lost? Is it really better, as the poet says, to have loved and lost than never to have loved at all? Is any amount of excitement and spiritual union worth the pain and grief of losing love?

There are many who believe that grief can lead to a deeper capacity for passion. As Kahlil Gibran says,

Your joy is your sorow unmasked.
And the selfsame well from which your laughter rises was oftentimes filled with your tears.
And how else can it be?
The deeper that sorrow carves into your being, the more joy you can contain.

LIFE AS CURRICULUM

Since each person's reality is what he or she chooses to make it based on perception and values, we like to choose those constructions that seem wise and useful.

One interesting perception is the idea that life is a series of lessons to be learned. How is it that a person struggles and finally leaves a traumatic relationship, only to choose an eerily similar one next time? How does the unconscious mind manage to see past the social facade and connect with a new mate whose core self is so similar to the one before?

We are continually awed by the uncanny way people's radar seems to work in finding each other. Perhaps people do indeed set up lessons they need to learn, and do them over and over, in amazingly creative variations, until the lesson is well and truly learned.

TENDING AND NURTURING LOVE

The heart connection that began the love affair needs to be nurtured, protected, and fondly maintained. This means telling each other what channel you receive Love on.

There once was a woman who said to her husband, "I don't feel loved any more. You used to bring me flowers, and now you never do." He was indignant. Didn't he change the oil on her car, and pick her up at the airport, and spend the whole day Sunday visiting her mother? Didn't he cuddle up to her at night, and tell her what a good cook she was? "Yes," she said sorrowfully, "but you don't bring me flowers any more."

Is she silly? What difference does it make? Flowers from her husband say "I love you" in a way her heart understands.

There was a man whose mother had been a housewife who had dinner waiting for her family every night promptly at six. He said to his wife, "A way I receive love is to sit down to a prepared meal and visit while we eat." Does it mean his working wife must dash home and start rattling pots and pans? Not at all. They both have a dozen places they can stop for take-out food when they're too overextended to even want to warm up leftovers—but most nights now they sit down to a set table, and they talk, and he feels loved and she feels loving.

We know a couple who value their slumber parties above all other activities that they share. Slumber parties, they say, are those spontantous happenings when they are too keyed up for sleep and instead lie awake and talk, and laugh, and sometimes sing old songs together. The woman says that slumber parties are the greatest aphrodisiac she knows, because they make her feel close to her husband. She feels cherished as a person.

According to the American Association for Marriage and Family Therapy, the average couple spends *less that 15 minutes a week* in intimate conversations. No wonder we have a society with well-maintained, effective machinery, and a 50% divorce rate. We change the oil on the car, clean out the lint filter on the dryer, empty the dishwasher, launder the clothes. We tend the things and not the people.

RETURN TO ROMANCE

Since they were married twelve years ago, about once a year Elaine and Phil pick each other up in a hotel bar. Out of the blue, one calls the other and says, "Sidetap Lounge, six-thirty." At the appointed hour they sit side by side at the bar, each sipping a cocktail and pretending not to know each other. Then one says to the other, "So, are you from around here?" or some other corny introductory phrase, and they begin to talk.

As each takes on a new persona for the evening, they listen closely to the fascinating story each has to tell. What emerges is not less intimacy than they usually have, but more, because by giving up their everyday roles *(Did you feed the dog? How's your dad doing? Where are we going to get the money for the income tax?)* they get to become more of who each person really is.

Perhaps that is the best definition of intimate conversation—talking about your Selves, not what you Do.

Even though he's only pretending to have grown up on a ranch in Montana, Phil tells Elaine about things that fascinate him. Perhaps she will surprise him some Saturday morning with a horseback riding date.

If Elaine imagines herself an actress living in a Manhattan penthouse, maybe she's really saying she's starved for a little glamour. Maybe he'll take her to a hotel rooftop restaurant some evening and buy her champagne, and perhaps even give her, in a velvet box, a bracelet of "diamonds."

THE WEEKLY DATE

The happiest couples we know have a standing date for at least one evening a week. Nothing short of a genuine emergency gets in the way of their date. They take turns planning what they'll do to delight the other one, though they've been known to spontaneously scrap that night's plan and just hang out, lingering over dinner or strolling through the twilight holding hands.

Rekindled romantic love can give you the heart and motivation to deal with inevitable problems in a respectful way. When you feel loved and loving, you are more likely to hear the other person with empathy and support, and trust that you can help the other without giving up yourself.

THE NEED FOR SPACE

Even the hottest fire needs air and oxygen or it will burn itself up. So it is with lovers—and some people have a stronger need for space than others. The wish to be alone for awhile or in the company of other friends is not a rejection of the beloved, it's simply a need for psychic recharging.

The German poet Rainer Maria Rilke wrote:

> *A good marriage is that in which each appoints the other guardian of his solitude. Once the realization is accepted that between the closest human beings infinite distances continue to exist, a wonderful living side by side can grow up, if they succeed in loving the distance between them which makes it possible for each to see the other whole against a wide sky.*

FRIENDS OF THE HEART

Most of us have a number of friends who receive our holiday cards, party invitations, birth announcements. But there is another depth of friendship that we share with very few people in an entire lifetime. A man tells this story.

> *I never knew I could love a friend the way I do Frank. When my wife was in the car wreck, Frank sat with me at the hospital while I waited to see what the doctors said. I had so many feelings, and Frank was like a rock while I poured them out. I was enraged at that drunk driver, and so*

scared she wouldn't make it. Then when I found out she was going to be completely okay, I was so relieved I cried.

Through all of that Frank stayed with me. He didn't say many words—he didn't have to. He just leaned in and really looked at me while he listened, and when I cried he did too.

I've always known I loved my dad and my brothers, but the bond I have with Frank is every bit as close as the one I have to blood kin.

Not long ago Frank and I were having dinner at a restaurant while our wives went to a meeting, and we were laughing so hard that people looked over at us and grinned. A lady stopped by our table on the way out and said, "You guys are having so much fun." Frank said, "Aren't we!" She asked if we were kinfolks, and so help me, Frank and I _both_ said, "Only in the heart."

THE TREE THAT BORE WOMEN

There are two women who met at a professional conference in San Francisco and knew immediately that they were going to be friends. After getting better acquainted over lunch, they decided to skip the last session, rent a car, and go see Muir Woods together.

They talked and walked through the woods, learning how they were alike and some of the ways they were different. They discovered that they both trusted their intuition and spontaneity, and that they felt a deep connection even after so short a time. They recalled the friendships they made with other girls at summer camp when they were adolescents, the confidences shared, pledges of undying closeness, letters that came and then stopped coming. They made a pact that even though they lived half a continent apart they would nurture their new friendship and make it thrive.

As they walked along the path among the ancient redwoods, the women spotted a large, very old tree that was split open and hollow. They walked over to it and squeezed inside, still feeling like girls at camp sharing an adventure.

Just then a young family came by, and the father said to his children, "Look, kids! That tree is bearing women!" Everyone laughed, and to the women it seemed a kind of blessing.

They kept their pact and have deepened the friendship. They visit each other when they can, write long letters at irregular intervals, and sometimes call and talk late into the night. They comfort each other in tough times and celebrate triumphs together. Wherever they are, each knows she has a place in the other's heart.

LIVING AS LOVING

You can't be truly alive and _not_ love others, whether in friendship or romantic love. It simply is not an option.

Love is like a balloon. Once it's been filled, it is always stretched. Even though it's deflated and wrinkled, it has more elasticity and a greater capacity for the next filling. What it fills with is more and more of Life with all its permutations—its frustration and dawn of understanding, its shadows and dazzling fragments of joy.

Kahlil Gibran says about Love:

But if in your fear you would seek only love's peace and love's pleasure,
Then it is better for you that you cover your nakedness and pass out of love's threshing-floor,
Into the seasonless world where you shall laugh, but not all of your laughter,
And weep, but not all of your tears.

CHAPTER 9

THE MIND / BODY CONNECTION

THE POWER OF PASSION

A few years ago, the story goes, jazz musician Dave Brubeck was desperately, perhaps terminally, ill and in terrible pain. Even so, he refused pain-deadening medications because he wanted to be fully alive as long as he had breath left. He asked for a keyboard to distract himself from the pain, and ended up creating some of the finest compositions of his career.

He also got well.

Passion can create its own healing grace.

THE MIND/BODY CONTINUUM

The mind and body are dancing in a circle, looping back upon themselves, each contributing to the programming of the other.

The word *psychsomatic* literally means *of the mind and body*. The term *psychogenic* means *born of the mind*. They both refer to the continual connection, communication, and interrelation of our bodies and our minds. Indeed, there is no separation between them.

THE BODY AS PROGRAMMER
Perhaps you have read of a physical therapy called "patterning" that is used to treat brain-injured patients who have lost their ability to walk. The patient is put on his stomach on the floor and the helpers move his arms and legs in a creeping manner, the way a baby begins his experiments with forward movement. Gradually the patient learns to creep, then crawl, then stand erect, and finally walk. It doesn't work all the time, but it helps in a great number of cases.

The body is reprogramming the brain to reprogram the body!

Another example of this phenomenon was discovered and developed dramatically by the late Moshe Feldenkrais. He was an Israeli physicist who held a black belt in judo, and after suffering a bad knee injury he became fascinated with the connections between mind and body. Using his knowledge of physics and judo, he literally taught himself to walk again.

From that experience he developed a series of thousands of movements designed to re-teach the body how to use itself better. He believed that we are limited by the ways we first learn to move as children, and we keep moving that way our whole lives unless we choose to re-educate ourselves.

Using his movements, cerebral palsied people have learned to use their bodies in ways they would never have thought possible. Crash victims have regained and sometimes surpassed their former abilities.

We patterned and wired our learning once, and we can do it again. By working directly and consciously with the nervous system, we can create new neural and muscular pathways.

THE MIND AS PROGRAMMER

It works the other way, too. We can consciously use the mind to influence the health of the body. Through the study of deliberate relaxation, people have learned to affect those body responses we used to call "autonomic." People can be taught how to lower their blood pressure, slow their own heartbeat, reduce their rate of respiration.

The formal name for such purposeful relaxation and clearing of the mind is meditation. In this day of high-tech medicine, there is a gentle irony in the fact that one of the most valuable tools for reducing stress is a practice which has been with us for thousands of years.

MEDITATION, THE WHOLESOME TRANQUILIZER

Millions of people all over the world regularly practice meditation. Yogis have for centuries been able to control their respiration, even the rate of their heartbeats, through meditation.

For thirty years Alan Watts has brought the principles of Eastern traditions to the notice of Westerners. As an early and articulate proponent of meditation, he wrote:

> *We are sick with a fascination for the useful tools of names and numbers, of symbols, signs, conceptions and ideas. Meditation is therefore the art of suspending verbal and symbolic thinking for a time, somewhat as a courteous audience will stop talking when a concert is about to begin.*

PSYCHONEUROIMMUNOLOGY, THE LINK-UP

The traditional view of the body as simply a machine is outmoded. The new field of psychoneuroimmunology is seen by many as the medicine of the future. It brings science, medicine, psychology, and spirituality together in the service of healing.

Studies in psychoneuroimmunology provide clear evidence that stress is detrimental to the immune system and can contribute to disease susceptibility. They also provide evidence that relaxation and meditation techniques can reverse these effects and return the body to a state of balance.

In China there are two kinds of medicine that exist side by side. One is the Western version, with pharmaceuticals and the "medical model." The other, called traditional medicine, presumes the presence of something called *"chi." Chi* is the essential energy of the body, and traditional practitioners believe that many illnesses are caused by an interruption of the normal flow of *chi,* a kind of roadblock that is interrupting internal harmony. To bring a patient's *chi* back into balance might require certain herbs brewed into a tea, as well as acupuncure or acupressure.

As they are in psychoneuroimmunology, the physical, emotional, and spiritual elements are all honored and often blended in China, with the result that high-tech surgeries may be performed with the attending anaesthetist using traditional acupuncture to anaesthetize the patient.

Bill Moyers created a PBS television series and best-selling book entitled Healing and the Mind. His research took him to China, and he says about that experience:

> *The Chinese look on the human being as a garden, as a living organism, with every part connected. Americans see the body as a machine.*
>
> *It isn't wrong, the body is a machine. But it's also a garden. We have to tend both.*

Such non-technical approaches to healing occur all over the planet. The New England Journal Of Medicine reports that more than sixty million people a year pursue options like massage, herbs, acupressure, and other nontraditional treatments for therapeutic purposes, but don't tell their physicians about it.

HEALING THE SPIRIT

Among healthcare experts who deal with grave illness there is a growing perception of a distinct difference between *curing* and *healing*. Healing is a process of acceptance, forgiveness, and release that can and does occur even for incurable patients.

Some people diagnosed with a terminal illness miraculously go into remission. Others do indeed die, but by choosing their perceptions and taking active part in their own treatment, they live longer than their prognoses indicated, and more importantly, they live better. Sometimes better than they ever have before.

Although they are not able to be cured, they are able to *heal* their lives and their minds. They have the experience of being able to choose how they will respond, instead of simply reacting in a knee-jerk manner as they perhaps have been doing all their lives.

TAKING CARE OF YOURSELF

Let's be realistic. There are such things as viruses and carcinogenic substances in our lives. Recently a research and clinical team isolated a bacterium now thought to be responsible for 60% of stomach cancer and virtually all duodenal ulcers, proving that such illnesses are not necessarily caused by stress, as previously believed. It would be dangerous, as well as cruel, to suggest that we "make ourselves sick" when such causative agents are at work.

The mind/body movement in medicine has no intention of blaming the patient for illness. It simply wants the patient to be involved and educated, not just a machine in need of fixing.

Dr. Bernard Siegel is world-reknown in his belief that it can, and he challenges us to adopt a new and healthier way of looking at life. In suggesting attitudes and actions to influence the outcome of an illness, he points out that it would be wise to learn these lessons <u>before</u> being diagnosed with a life-threatening illness.

These are the steps Bernie Siegel suggests the patient follow, to be proactive in his or her own healing process.

1) *<u>Don't be afraid to show your vulnerabilities.</u>*
Acting one way when you're feeling another, putting on a "brave front" no matter what, pulls down our vitality. We end up with fewer friends and little support when we're always trying to tough it out. Asking for help is not an admission of weakness, and neither is telling the truth to a friend when you feel lousy.

2) *<u>Relinquish your need to be in control.</u>*
The old to-do list can cease to be a helpful tool and become a tyrant, if you let it. Life was never intended to be orderly, and living well means being judicious about when to live with a rigid schedule and when not to. Bernie Siegel says, "Living well ... means learning to find happiness, fulfillment and tranquility in the face of disorder. ...Make plans, but don't be upset by redirection. Something good may come of this redirection."

3) *<u>Learn how to say "no."</u>*
Again, Bernie Siegel: "Saying Yes when you'd rather say No may be good manners, but it's destructive to our health. It leads us to do things we detest, and it

distracts us from the things we cherish. ...I'm not asking you to be selfish or needlessly rude. I'm merely asking you to have enough self-esteem to stand up for yourself, to pursue life on your own terms, to realize that you can say No when someone asks you to change your plans."

4) *Confront your fears.*

People in crisis often seek peace of mind through the process of denial, when it is confronting our fears that creates real power. Once you have defined your fear concretely, find a way to comfort and reassure it, as you would a scared little kid. Acknowledge the fear and nurture yourself, instead of trying to be "brave" and burying it. It will always surface anyway, so you might as well incorporate it into the reality of your being.

5) *Live in the moment.*

If you can approach life with a childlike sense of awe and wonder, you'll really *live* each moment, not just tick it off. It is possible to see a life-threatening illness as a *wake-up call to life.* How infinitely better it is to wake up now, before an illness gets our attention.

6) *Identify your true wishes.*

Helen Keller, blind and deaf from infancy, taught herself to tune in to her deepest wishes. She used to ask herself,

> *If you had three days to see,
> what would you choose to see
> in those days?*

By asking yourself similar questions, you can learn more about what you truly love in your life.

7) <u>Refuse to be a victim.</u>
Empowerment comes through realizing that you cannot control what happens to you, but you can choose how you will respond to it. This is the truth: You are never really in control of life. That truck can blindside you at any moment. You are, however, wholly and absolutely in charge of how you will choose to respond.

GLENN'S DREAM
When Glenn was diagnosed with inoperable prostate cancer, he was determined to defeat it. He'd worked hard to get his life together and was succeeding. He was reconnecting with his grown children and his wife, and for the first time in his memory was starting to feel his authentic power.

As part of his therapy he was advised to give himself permission to remember his dreams.

This is the dream he had just before beginning radiation treatments.

I am at the top of a long spiral staircase. Going down through the middle of the staircase is a milky column in which lights continually flicker upward, changing color as they go.

I begin to descend the steps. When I get to the bottom I am in a kind of courtyard in which there are five flames, each in an Olympics-type brazier.

I visit each one in turn. I am able to put my hand into each flame—they are a kind of fire which gives warmth but does not burn. I sense that each one has a different gift for me, but I don't know what it is.

For several weeks, each time Glenn came for counseling he told about a new variation on the dream. In his second dream the staircase and column were the same as before, but this time he floated down the steps. Next time, the lights ascending within the column had become more complex and more beautiful. Next, he realized that the top of the staircase was in the clouds.

He conjectured with his counselor about the meaning of the messages he was sending himself through these creative metaphors. Sometimes the staircase reminded him of the DNA molecule. Certainly the fires represented, at the very least, the radiation which was designed to heal and not burn, at least not much.

One day he said with uncharacteristic excitement, "The fires are fuel, and the staircase is a spaceship."

And finally, *"I am the spaceship. The fires are **my fuel**!"*

Glenn <u>was</u> beating his cancer—but his heart, damaged from other illnesses, gave out on him one morning in his kitchen.

At his memorial service, his counselor told the story of Glenn and his healing fires. Everyone there understood. Even though Glenn did not have a chance to get fully cured, he healed himself with those fires of his spirit before he died.

HEALING YOUR EMOTIONS

It is not just our bodies that need caretaking immune systems. Our feelings do too.

Since we are taught from early childhood to analyze problems and find solutions, it's easy to confuse the <u>origin</u> of a problem with <u>blame.</u> It is easier to heal a broken leg than a shattered self-esteem, yet we often blame and punish ourselves for events long in the past, for people's behavior that we had no control over.

Self-esteem means just that: *to hold oneself in esteem, to respect oneself.*

It includes old-fashioned compassion. You wouldn't indict a child for having tried something and finding out it didn't work very well. Why not extend the same respect to yourself?

THE MAGICAL SYSTEM

Norman Cousins has written extensively about the power of inner perspective to affect physical health.

The greatest force in the human body is the natural drive of the body to heal itself—but that force is not independent of the belief system, which can translate expectations into physiological change. Nothing is more wondrous about the fifteen billion neurons in the human brain than their ability to convert thoughts, hopes, ideas, and attitudes into chemical substances.

Everything begins, therefore, with belief. What we believe is the most powerful option of all.

CHAPTER 10

COMING ALIVE !

*You are a child of the universe.
No less than the trees and the stars,
you have a right to be here.*
— **Desiderata**

THE SCIENTIST'S ASTONISHMENT

Have you ever stopped to think what a miracle it is that you <u>are</u> here?

In his book <u>The Lives of a Cell</u> biologist and physician Lewis Thomas celebrates all life on the planet from a scientist's viewpoint. He writes:

> *Statistically, the probability of any one of us being here is so small that you'd think the mere fact of existing would keep us all in a contented dazzlement of surprise. We are alive against the stupendous odds of genetics, infinitely outnumbered by all the alternatives who might, except for luck, be in our places.*
>
> *... We violate probability, by our nature. To be able to do this systematically, and in such wild varieties of form, from viruses to whales, is extremely unlikely; to have sustained the effort successfully for several billion years of our existence, without drifting back into randomness, was nearly a mathematical impossibility.*
>
> *Add to this the biological improbability that makes each member of our own species unique. Everyone is one in three billion at the moment, which describes the odds.*
>
> *Each of us is a self-contained, free-standing individual, labeled by specific protein configurations at the surfaces of cells, identifiable by whorls of fingertip skin, maybe even by special medleys of fragrance. You'd think we'd never stop dancing.*

This sense of awe and wonder, celebration and appreciation is the key to the passion we call *joie de vivre*—lifelove.

LIVING RIGHT, NOW

One of the most firmly embedded habits most of us have is living in the nostalgic or regretful past *(Wasn't it great?* or *If only I'd...)* or in the future *(I'll be happy when...)* but not in the present.

To live a vibrant, empassioned life requires that you

> *BE HERE NOW!*

It's something we all knew as little kids, but somehow lost touch with in the process of becoming super-responsible adults.

Our western society rewards us for planning ahead, setting and meeting goals, and visualizing the future—activities that are necessary and desirable in certain settings. But the price is terrible when we misplace the ability to savor life and the moment, right now.

Being present-conscious is a skill that can be learned. Like all skills, it becomes easier and eventually automatic through practice.

You have learned so very many skills in your life, abilities you now think nothing of. You can also master the skill of being more present-centered, more fully alive.

TAKE A CELEBRATION BREAK!

This is what it is like. You'll be going along in automatic autopilot, tending to tasks, checking off the to-do list, when you *notice that you haven't been noticing.* At the appropriate moment you purposefuly choose to take a break from your left-brain fast-tracking. As the saying goes, you wake up and smell the coffee.

You take a break to celebrate the fact of existence. You celebrate your body (stretch a little and feel its presence). You celebrate your mind. You celebrate your spirit. You celebrate the life force that is handed down, one generation to another, to all the plants and creatures of the earth. You feel a stirring of gratitude, a sense of the beautiful harmony that exists between your reason and your passion, and it builds into the *YES!* that is thankfulness for life and relationships and sensibilities.

Kahlil Gibran wrote:

Therefore let your soul exalt your reason to the height of passion, that it may sing;
And let it direct your passion with reason, that your passion may live through its own daily resurrection, and like the phoenix rise above its own ashes.
I would have you consider your judgment and your appetite even as you would two loved guests in your house.

Surely you would not honour one guest above the other; for he who is more mindful of one loses the love and faith of both.

Among the hills, when you sit in the cool shade of the white poplars, sharing the peace and serenity of distant fields and meadows—then let your heart say in silence, "God rests in reason."

And when the storm comes, and the mighty wind shakes the forest, and thunder and lightning proclaim the majesty of the sky—then let your heart say in awe, "God moves in passion."

And since you are a breath in God's sphere, and a leaf in God's forest, you too should rest in reason and move in passion.

> *May you rest in reason
> and move in passion
> all the days of your life.*

EXERCISES FOR

RECLAIMING PASSION

Whether you are travelling the Paths of Passion by yourself, with a partner, or in a support group, here are some questions and activities that may help you on your way. Notice what happens inside yourself as you look at these exercises. Recognition? Resistance? Delight? Whatever comes up, honor it. It's your unconscious Self sending you a message about your comfort level.

When answering the questions, let your pen write spontaneously, as if the flow of responses were going straight from your heart to your fingers without getting sidetracked by the critic in your head. The first thing that occurs to you, unedited, often comes from a deep internal wisdom. You might want to explore some of your responses further by keeping a journal.

Just do the exercises you want to. Later on you can decide whether the others are a stretch you're ready to take, or perhaps are just not relevant to you.

Activities for
PATH #1
HONORING YOURSELF

Do you find that setting respectful but clear boundaries on others *or on yourself* leaves you feeling guilty? Ask yourself this:

What messages am I sending myself that are producing this uneasiness? Am I telling myself things like ...

> "You ought to be ashamed of yourself, ducking out on your responsibilities like that."

> "I shouldn't be taking time to fool with this guitar now—I still haven't planned my appointments for next week (haven't folded the clothes, haven't phoned Mother, haven't haven't haven't)."

Instead of being your biggest critic, maybe you could start trying to be your own friend. Once you have made a sincere effort at accomplishing tasks or accommodating others, cut yourself some slack! Isn't that the counsel you would give another friend? Have a little empathy for yourself.

The Compassion Model

You have an experience, followed by your interpretation of its meaning; then you can <u>react</u> automatically or choose to <u>respond</u>.

SHAME/BLAME REACTION vs. COMPASSION RESPONSE

Process	**Process**
Judge (self &/or other)	Understanding (self &/or other)
Blame	Release

Outcome	**Outcome**
Anger / Guilt / Bondage	Love / Freedom / Hope

Spinoffs	**Spinoffs**
Stagnation	Increased Creativity
Disillusionment	Passion
Repetition	Learning the lesson
Cynicism	Purpose

It increases peace of mind and makes better sense to appreciate life, learning, and intent, rather than indict yourself or others.

Activities for
PATH #2
CLAIMING YOUR AUTHENTIC POWER

These are steps for paying attention to your own inner signals and <u>responding</u> to a situation instead of just <u>reacting</u>. These steps are a model for honest assertiveness that allows you to respect yourself and the other person.

1) **Be Aware**

    — of your *feelings*
      ("That doesn't feel good / right."
      "I feel gypped."
      "I feel unsafe.")

    — of your *self-talk*
      "I wish they'd do it <u>my</u> way—it's the <u>right</u> way."
      "If s/he loved me, s/he would <u>know</u>
        (how to please me) (what I want) (how I feel)."
      "Well, I couldn't help it. After all, I'm just ..."

2) **Hit Your Pause Button**

Stop a moment to interrupt your Automatic Autopilot reaction. Buy a little time. Say to the other person or yourself, "I want to think about that and get back to you."

3) **Consider**

What's really going on? Is my Self-Talk useful feedback or old, lousy programming?

Am I giving my power away, being a victim or a martyr? Or ducking out on responsibility?

What are the various ways I could respond here [identify alternatives].

Which one(s) seem best? Is that option respectful to everyone, including myself?

4) **Choose and Act**

Choose an alternative to try out.

Check back with your gut, recycle till it feels right, then act on it.

If it doesn't work out as you'd anticipated, learn from that and try again.

Questions for
PATH #3
EXPANDING YOUR COMFORT ZONE

In his book <u>Risking</u> psychiatrist David Viscott offers these questions to help you assess the risk/benefit ratio in stretching your Comfort Zone.

RISK TRACK-DOWN

1) Is this risk necessary?

2) Can I reach my goal in another way?

3) Is the potential loss greater than the possible gain?

4) What do I need to know before taking this risk?

5) Who can tell me what I need to know?

6) Who wants me to succeed at this risk?

7) Who secretly wants me to fail at this risk?

8) What part should I let these sources play in my life?

9) Who else can profit by this risk?

10) Who else can lose by this risk?

11) Am I afraid? Afraid of what?

12) Am I ready to act? If not now, when?

Exercises for Reclaiming Passion

Activity for
PATH #4
FOLLOWING YOUR BLISS

In his book <u>Keeping the Love You Find</u> Harville Hendrix recommends a Self-Knowledge Inventory. Here are some of the questions he suggests you ask yourself.

1. The thing that gives me the most satisfaction is ....
   ....

2. My idea of a dream career is ....
   ....

3. When I have spare time, I like to ....
   ....

4. I am afraid of ....
   ....

5. In general, I view life as ....
   ....

6. When I grow old ....
   ....

*NOW, HOW ABOUT MAKING
A <u>TO-BE LIST</u> FOR YOURSELF?*

Exercise for
PATH #5
AFFIRMING THE YES! TO LIFE

PASSION PERMISSIONS

Permission for passion is a fundamental issue in our ability to enjoy life. If either from the past or from ourselves we do not have permission to allow and even cultivate our passion, we're stymied.

What are some messages, direct or indirect, that you received?

Encouraging messages from father or father figure

Exercises for Reclaiming Passion

Encouraging messages from mother or mother figure

Discouraging messages from father or father figure

Discouraging messages from mother or mother figure

[   ]

After this review of your past programming, which messages, beliefs, attitudes do you want to keep or discard, and what new permissions do you want to install?

Passion Permissions from Myself

1. ....

2. ....

3. ....

4. ....

5. ....

Exercise for
PATH #6
TRUSTING YOUR
INNER CLICK

Read through this exercise once. Then read through it again. Then get comfortable and let yourself have the experience.

KAIROTIC KNOWING

Allow yourself to remember a time when you had a flash of intuition, an inner click of <u>Yes</u>! about a person, a job choice, an event—<u>you just knew</u> that it fit for you. Let yourself feel that physical memory in your body. What was your most noticeable emotion. Excitement? Quiet intensity? Hyper-awareness?

Now focus on a challenge you are having in your current life. Close your eyes and beathe slowly and deeply. Now ask yourself:

>What is my inner sense of knowing?
>Is this the right time?
>Are these the right people?

Your answers come from deep within your internal knowing. Trust them.

Exercise for
PATH #7
UNITING YOUR HEAD AND HEART

THE RULES FOR BEING HUMAN
—Anonymous

1. **YOU WILL RECEIVE A BODY.**
   You may like it or hate it, but it will be yours for the entire period of time.

2. **YOU WILL LEARN LESSONS.**
   You are enrolled in a full-time informal school called Life. Each day in this school you will have the opportunity to learn lessons. You may like the lessons or think them irrelevent and stupid.

3. **THERE ARE NO MISTAKES, ONLY LESSONS.**
   Growth is a process of trial and error: *experimentation*. The "failed" experiments are as much a part of the process as the experiment that ultimately "works."

4. **A LESSON IS REPEATED UNTIL YOU LEARN IT.**
   A lesson will be presented to you in various forms until you have learned it. When you have learned it, you can then go on to the next lesson.

5. **LEARNING LESSONS DOES NOT END.**
   There is no part of life that does not contain its lessons. If you are alive, there are lessons to be learned.

6. **"THERE" IS NO BETTER THAN "HERE"**
   When your "there" has become a "here," you will simply obtain another "there" that will again look better than "here."

7. **OTHERS ARE MERELY MIRRORS OF YOU.**
   You cannot love or hate something about another person unless it reflects something you love or hate about yourself.

8. **WHAT YOU MAKE OF YOUR LIFE IS UP TO YOU.**
   You have all the tools and resources you need. What you do with them is up to you. The choice is yours.

9. **YOUR ANSWERS LIE INSIDE YOU.**
   The answers to Life's questions lie inside you. All you need to do is look, listen and trust.

10. **YOU WILL FORGET ALL THIS.**

11. **YOU CAN REMEMBER IT WHENEVER YOU WANT.**

Exercise: If you knew you had only six months left of your life, what would you do? Who would say "I love you" to? What changes would you make in your daily life? How would you spend your remaining time? The answers can show you how to unite your head and heart and purposefully choose—*right now*.

As a final exercise, we invite you to read this passage from Lewis Thomas's <u>Medusa and the Snail</u> and ponder it lovingly in your mind and spirit:

You start out as a single cell derived from the coupling of a sperm and an egg; this divides into two, then four, then eight, and so on, and at a certain stage there emerges a single cell which will have as all its progeny the human brain.

The mere existence of that cell should be one of the great astonishments of the earth. ...It is an unbelievable thing, and yet there it is, popping neatly into its place amid the jumbled cells of every one of the several billion human embryos around the planet, just as if it were the easiest thing in the world to do.

If you like being surprised, there's the source. One cell is switched on to become the whole trillion-cell, massive apparatus for thinking and imagining, and, for that matter, for being surprised. All the information needed for learning to read and write, playing the piano, arguing before senatorial sub-committees, walking across a street through traffic, or the marvelous human act of putting out one hand and leaning against a tree, is contained in that first cell. All of grammar, all syntax, all arithmetic, all music. ...

No one has the ghost of an idea how this works, and nothing else in life can ever be so puzzling. If anyone does succeed in explaining it within my lifetime, I will charter a skywriting airplane, maybe a whole fleet of them, and send them aloft to write one great exclamation point after another, around the whole sky, until all my money runs out.

Roz Van Meter, MA Biography

Roz Van Meter used to get sent to detention for reading library books in class—which was all right with her, because she got to finish reading them in detention.

It was a short haul from all that reading (an addiction which persists till today) to the love of writing. After a career ranging from television to advertising copywriting, she became a mid-life graduate student, emerging with a masters degree in communication in human relations and doctoral work in counseling psychology.

The resulting career change led first to academia (she has been on the faculty of three colleges), then her Dallas counseling practice (for the past seventeen years), consultant work, and dozens of training seminars and workshops. She also appeared for six months as a regular guest editor on an ABC-affiliate television talk show.

Roz is the author of several books, including <u>Life Savor: How to Turn on Delight</u>—a self-help book for living life with appreciation for self and others regardless of early or current difficulties—and <u>More Power to You</u>, about techniques for identifying and removing blocks to self-esteem and intimacy.

She is a licensed professional counselor, licensed marriage and family therapist, and AASECT-certified sex therapist. In seminars as well as private counseling, her colorful style is always results-oriented. She combines a study of the powerful impact of family and cultural myths and stories with present-day, pragmatic how-to's for creating a satisfying life.

Roz is a dynamic and entertaining speaker on a wide spectrum of subjects from passionate living to re-engagement in marriage to family and organizational system dynamics.

She is the mother of three grown children and enjoys exuberant, passionate lifelove with photographer Robert Goodman.

PAT PEARSON, MSSW
BIOGRAPHY

Pat Pearson is a charismatic speaker with a real passion for inspiring audiences to claim their own personal excellence.

Pat has for ten years been a widely acclaimed and requested presenter. She travels across the country sharing ideas on personal and professional development, sales psychology, stress reduction, and employee productivity with many of the world's leading companies, including IBM, Mary Kay Cosmetics, Travelers Insurance, Century 21, Southwestern Bell Telephone, and Hunt Oil Company. Her powerful keynote speeches and seminars are informative as well as entertaining, and she consistently receives standing ovations, highest audience ratings, and continual requests for repeat engagements. Unlike mere "motivational" speakers, she provides concrete behavioral methods for mobilizing the audience's inner resources.

Pat graduated from Southern Methodist University and received her Masters in Social Work from the University of Texas at Arlington. Prior to forming Pearson Presentations, she was a Dallas psychotherapist.

She is author of <u>You Deserve the Best</u>, in which she provides a blueprint on how to stop self-sabotage and deserve more, then offers proven methods for sustaining this higher level of deserving.

Pat is a member of the National Speakers Association, Executive Women of Dallas, Meeting Planners International, and the Dallas Women's Foundation. She was appointed by former Texas governor Mark White to the Texas State Speaker's Bureau. For her personal and professional accomplishments she was selected to be in Who's Who in American Women.

READING LIST

Many of these readings are referred to in this text. Others are books we have found enlightening over the years. We are grateful to all the authors for their wisdom and insight.

Borysenko, Joan. *Guilt Is the Teacher, Love is the Lesson.* New York: Warner Books, Inc., 1990.

Borysenko, Joan. *Minding the Body, Mending the Mind.* New York: Bantam Books, 1988.

Bradshaw, John. *Healing the Shame that Binds You.* Deerfield Beach: Health Communications, Inc., 1988.

Branden, Nathaniel. *The Psychology of Self-Esteem.* Los Angeles: Nash Publishing Corporation, 1969.

Branden, Nathaniel. *Honoring the Self.* Los Angeles: Jeremy P. Tarcher, Inc., 1983.

Brazelton, T. Berry, M.D. *What Every Baby Knows.* Reeding, MA: Addison Wesley Publishing, 1987.

Buber, Martin. *I and Thou.* New York: Charles Scribner's Sons, 1970.

Campbell, Joseph, with Bill Moyers. *The Power of Myth.* New York, Doubleday, 1988.

Carse, James P. *Finite and Infinite Games.* New York: Ballentine Books, 1986.

Cousins, Norman. *Anatomy of an Illness.* New York: Bantam Books, 1979.

Csikszentmihalyi, Mihaly. *Flow: The Psychology of Optimal Experience.* New York: Harper Perennial Press, 1990.

cummings, e.e. *Complete Poems 1913-1962.* New York: Harcourt Brace Jovanovich, 1923-1963.

Dennis, Patrick. *Auntie Mame.* New York: Vanguard Press, Inc., 1955.

Dillard, Annie. *Pilgrim at Tinker Creek.* New York: Perennial Library, Harper & Row, 1974.

Eliot, T.S. *The Waste Land and Other Poems.* New York: Harvest Books, 1962.

Faber, Adele and Mazlish, Elaine. *How To Talk So Kids Will Listen and Listen So Kids Will Talk.* New York: Avon, 1990.

Farnham, Alan. "Mary Kay's Lessons in Leadership," *Fortune*, 20 September 1993, pages 68-77.

Feldenkrais, Moshe. *Awareness through Movement.* New York: Harper & Row, 1972.

Fields, Rick, with Peggy Taylor, Rex Weyler, and Rick Ingrasci. *Chop Wood, Carry Water: A Guide to Finding Spiritual Fulfillment in Everyday Life.* Los Angeles: Jeremy P. Tarcher, Inc., 1984

Frankl, Victor. *Man's Search for Meaning.* New York: Pocket Books, 1959.

Fulghum, Robert L. *All I Really Need to Know I Learned in Kindergarten.* New York: Ivy/Ballentine Books, 1989.

Gibran, Kahlil. *The Prophet.* New York: Alfred A. Knopf, 1923 &1951

Hawking, Stephen W. *A Brief History of Time.* New York: Bantam Books, 1988

Helprin, Mark. *Winter's Tale.* New York: Harcourt Brace Jovanovich, 1983.

Hendrix, Harville. *Getting the Love You Want.* New York: Henry Holt & Co., 1988.

Hendrix, Harville. *Keeping the Love You Find.* New York: Pocket Books, 1992.

Herbert, Anne. *Random Kindness and Senseless Acts of Beauty.* Volcano, CA: Volcano Press/Kazan Books, 1993.

Herbert, Frank. *Dune.* New York: Berkley Medallion Books, 1965.

Holt, John. *How Children Fail.* Philadelphia: Pitman Transatlantic Publishing, 1964.

Huff, Benjamin. *The Tao of Pooh.* Middlesex, England: Penguin Books Ltd., 1982.

James, Muriel. *Passion for Life.* New York: Dutton Press, 1991.

Jampolsky, Gerald. *Love Is Letting Go of Fear.* Millbrae, CA: Celestial Arts, 1979.

Jeffers, Susan. *Feel the Fear and Do It Anyway.* New York: Fawcett Columbine, 1987.

Jenkins, Dan. *Life Its Ownself.* New York: Simon and Schuster, 1984.

Jung, Carl G. *Man and His Symbols.* New York: Doubleday, 1964.

Kanin, Garson. *Tracy and Hepburn.* New York: Viking Press, 1971.
Kanin, Garson. *It Takes a Long Time to Become Young.* New York: Doubleday and Company, 1978.
Kazantzakis, Nikos. *Zorba the Greek.* New York: Simon and Schuser, 1952.
Keen, Sam. *To a Dancing God: Notes of a Spiritual Traveler.* Harper San Francisco. 1970.
Keller, Helen.*Teacher Anne Sullivan Macy: A Tribute by the Foster Child of Her Mind.* New York: Doubleday, 1955.
Keller, Helen. *Out of the Dark.* New York: Doubleday, 1914.
King, Alexander. *Mine Enemy Grows Older.* New York: Simon and Schuster, 1958.
L'Engle, Madelyn. *A Wrinkle in Time.* Berkeley: Ariel Books, 1962.
Lerner, Harriet G. *The Dance of Anger.* New York: Harper and Row (Perennial Library), 1986.
Mandel, Bob. *Open Heart Therapy.* Berkeley: Celestial Arts, 1984.
Matthiesson, Peter. *The Snow Leopard.* New York: Viking Press, 1978.
McWilliams, John-Roger and Peter. *The Portable Life 101.* Los Angeles: Prelude Press, 1992.
Moyers, Bill. *Healing and the Mind.* New York: Doubleday, 1993.
O'Keeffe, Georgia and Pollitzer, Anita (Clive Giboire, editor). *Lovingly, Georgia.* New York: Touchstone/Simon & Schuster, 1990.
Orwell, George.*1984.* San Diego: Harcourt Brace & World, 1949
Peck, M. Scott. *The Road Less Traveled: A New Psychology of Love, Traditional Values and Spiritual Growth.* New York: Touchstone Books, Simon and Schuster, 1978.
Piper, Watty (pseud).*The Little Engine That Could.* New York: Platt & Munk, 1961.
Powell, John. *Why Am I Afraid to Tell You Who I Am?* Allen, TX: Argus Communications, 1969.
Prather, Hugh. *A Book of Games.* New York: Doubleday, 1981.
Rilke, Rainer Maria.*Prose and Poetry.* New York: Continuum, 1984.
Rusk, Thomas. *Instead of Therapy.* Carson, CA: Hay House, 1991.
Sagan, Carl. *Cosmos.* Random House, New York, 1980.
Shain, Merle. *Courage My Love.* Bantam Books, New York, 1989.

Sher, Barbara, and Gottlieb, Annie. *Wishcraft*. New York, Viking Press, 1979.
Siegel, Bernie S., M.D. *Peace, Love and Healing*. New York: Harper and Row, 1989.
Thomas, Lewis. *The Lives of a Cell*. New York: Viking Press, 1974
Thomas, Lewis. *Medusa and the Snail*. New York: Viking Press, 1979.
Thomas, Peter. *Never Fight with a Pig: A Survival Guide for Entrepeneurs*. Toronto: Macmillan Canada, 1991.
Thoreau, Henry David. *Walden Pond*. W. W. Norton & Co., 1951
Van Meter, Roz. *Life Savor: How to Turn on Delight*. Dallas: Hollingsworth Press, 1987.
Viscott, David. *Risking*. New York: Pocket Books, 1977.
Walker, Alice. *The Color Purple*. San Diego: Harcourt-Brace-Javonovich, 1982.
Watts, Alan. *The Book on the Taboo Against Knowing Who You Are*. New York: Random House, 1989.
When I Am an Old Woman I Shall Wear Purple: An Anthology of Short Stories and Poems. Manhattan Beach, CA: Papier-Mache Press, 1987.
Whitsett, Gavin. *Guerrilla Kindness*. San Luis Obispo, CA: Impact Publishers, 1993.
Williams, Paul. *Das Energi*. New York: Warner Books, 1973,
Williamson, Marianne. *A Return to Love*. New York: Harper Perennial,1993.
Witkin, Georgia. *Passions*. New York: Villard Books, 1992.
Zukav, Gary. *The Seat of the Soul*. New York: Simon & Schuster, 1990.

INDEX

Addictive Behaviors, 30, 42
Alcoholics Anonymous, 93
ALD, 57
ALS, 106
Anti-Passion Devices, 40
Anti-Passion Results, 43
Ash, Mary Kay, 55
Auntie Mame, 21, 22
Bly, Robert, 41
Bradshaw, John, 42
Brazelton, T. Berry, 35
Brinker, Nancy, 53
Campbell, Joseph, 60, 114
Celestial Pearl, 128
Chemistry of Love, 154
Chi, 168
Churchill, Winston, 51
Cousins, Norman, 175
Csikszentmihalyi, Mihaly, 22, 48
cummings, e.e., 122, 151
Depression, 15,
Dillard, Annie, 67
Earhart, Amelia, 111
Feldenkrais, Moshe, 166
Flow, 48
Fulghum, Robert, 80
Gibran, Kahlil, 157, 164, 180
Gordon, Ruth, 156
Hawking, Stephen, 106
Healthy Passion Results, 29
Healthy Passion, 27
Helprin, Mark, 68
Hendrix, Harville, 154
Hepburn, Katherine, 64
Herbert, Anne, 120
Herbert, Frank, 105

Holt, John, 103
Huff, Benjamin, 66
Hundredth Monkey, 135
Hyperniceness, 41
James, Muriel, 123
Jenkins, Dan, 61
Kairos, 134, 139
Kanin, Garson, 156
Keen, Sam, 134
Keller, Helen, 100, 172
King, Alexander, 129
Komen, Susan G. Foundation, 54
Komen, Susan, 53
L'Engle, Madelyn, 39
LifeSavor, 143
Logan, Jim, 114
Lorenzo's Oil, 57
Magical Properties, 76, 78
Marci's Sky-Dive, 108
Meditation, 168
Michener, James, 149
Moyers, Bill, 168
O'Keeffe, Georgia, 138
Orwell, George, 39
Passion Permissions, 190
Plumb, Charles, 52
Psychoneuroimmunology, 168
Random Kindness, 120
Rilke, Rainer Maria, 161
Risking, 188
Rogers, Carl, 65
Sagan, Carl, 47
Seven Paths to Passion, 71
Shain, Merle, 147
Siegel, Bernard, 170-173
Singin' in the Rain, 19

INDEX

Special Olympics, 19, 20
Sullivan, Annie, 100
Twelve Steps of Non-Recovery, 93
Thomas, Lewis, 178, 196
Thomas, Peter, 139
Thoreau, Henry David, 146
Truman, Harry, 91
Van Gogh, Vincent, 48
Viscott, David, 188
Walker, Alice, 67
Watts, Alan, 168
Williams, Paul, 70
Williamson, Marianne, 13, 17
Witkins, Georgia, 31, 32
Zorba the Greek, 20, 21, 22
Zukav, Gary, 86